Manifesting

A Planning System
for Visual, Creative & Spiritual People

Also by Zorica Gojkovic

The Workings of Energy in the Human Energy Field: A Psychic's Perspective
Healing Relationships: A Guided Meditation
Healing Core Energies: A Guided Meditation
Evening Peace: A Guided Meditation
Relax, Let Go: A Guided Meditation
Morning Light: A Guided Meditation
Attunement: Daily Meditation
Affirmations of Highest Truth: A Guided Meditation

Manifesting

A Planning System
for Visual, Creative & Spiritual People

Zorica Gojkovic, Ph.D.

The Time of Light Productions

Copyright © 2019 by Zorica Gojkovic. All rights reserved.

No part of this book may be reproduced in any written, electronic, recording, or photocopying without express written permission of the publisher or author. The exception would be in the case of brief quotations embodied in the critical articles and reviews and pages where permission is specifically granted by the publisher or author.

Neither the publisher nor the author is engaged in rendering professional advice or services to the individual reader. The ideas, procedures, and suggestions contained in this book are not intended as a substitute for consulting with a health-care professional. All matters regarding your health require medical supervision. Neither the author nor the publisher shall be liable or responsible for any loss or damage allegedly arising from any information or suggestion in this book.

While the author and publisher have made every effort to ensure that the information in this book was correct at press time, the author and publisher do not assume and do hereby disclaim any liability to any party for any loss, damage, or disruption caused by errors or omissions, whether such errors or omissions result from negligence, accident, or any other cause.

Library of Congress Catalog Number: 2019900961
Print ISBN: 978-1-947168-02-2
eBook ISBN: 978-1-947168-03-9
The Time of Light Productions
www.thetimeoflight.com

*To all creative and spiritual people.
Stay strong!*

Acknowledgments

I would like to thank Athena Marshall and Nathaniel Rastallis for their valuable feedback.

Always on my mind is infinite gratitude to the greats: Jane Roberts, Robert Butts, Robert Monroe, Carlos Castaneda, Shakti Gawain, Sanaya Roman, and many others, who have contributed enormously to our understanding of the nature of reality and consciousness.

Contents

Preface / xvii

Introduction: A Planning & Manifesting System That Takes into Account All Aspects of Reality / 1

1. Your Thoughts & Beliefs Create Your Reality / 11

2. You Are Happiest When You Create from Your Soul Truth / 19

3. Establish a Strong Connection with Your Divine Self / 37

4. What Kinds of Things Can You Manifest? / 51

5. What Would You Like to Manifest? Let's Start Planning! / 59

6. The Planning System & How It Works / 67

7. Let's Manifest & Get Things Done! / 77

8. Be Willing to Change, Be Willing to Receive a Grander Life / 99

9. Parting Words / 113

A Meditation / 117

The Planning System Quick Reference Guide / 120

Supporting Material / 123

About the Author / 127

Manifesting

A Planning System
for Visual, Creative & Spiritual People

"For life is whatever we perceive it to be,
And freedom more than we ever conceived that it is,
And as we perceive we create our perception
For we are the creators and the creation."

From the poem, "Father," Zorica Gojkovic, 1979

Preface

What do you want? A loving relationship? Money? A great career? Excellent health? Do you feel lost and want to find your true path in life? Are things bugging you, but you don't know how to make them better? Are you seeking spiritual mastery?

Whatever it is you want, I will show you how to get it.

Many of us don't have what we want simply because we don't know how to get it. We may lack knowledge about how to plan effectively or how universal principles work to drive manifestation and, therefore, can't make use of that power.

In this short, easy-to-read book, I will show you how these universal principles operate. And I will show you a simple planning system based on these universal principles.

The Planning System will:
- Help you get clear on what you want in life
- Organize you so you know what action to take
- Show you how to use universal principles to manifest

This book is the answer to a life-long search about how the universe works and how our physical reality connects to spiritual reality.

For me, finding the answers to these questions was finding the magic key that unlocked all life's mysteries. Surprisingly, I discovered it when I started giving psychic readings.

It is ancient knowledge that everything is energy and that we create with our minds, our thoughts. The magic key, that unlocked everything for me, is seeing psychically how that energy operates in the human aura to create our reality and how that connects to the divine.

The purpose of this book is to show you how to use this magic key to create what you desire and to change unhappy life situations for the better. In this way, you can begin to feel your true power, the power of your soul and the fundamental love and support of the divine.

Introduction:

A Planning & Manifesting System That Takes into Account All Aspects of Reality

All my life I struggled with, well, organizing my life! Yes, organizing my life. Have you had the same problem?

I had dreams of things I yearned to create, changes I wanted to make and tasks I needed to get done. However, making all these things happen was always an awkward process of starts and stops, of random action with long periods of inaction, filled with anguish and frustration. Getting anything done at all was such an ordeal that, really, it was easier to do nothing than go through all that pain and turmoil. When I did accomplish things, they were a long time in coming and, in retrospect, should have required far less effort and certainly far less time.

Of course, I made lists. They didn't work because they were linear. They also didn't work because they were somewhere . . . where I'd forget all about them and, once out of sight, they were out of mind, literally.

Calendaring things didn't work for similar reasons. Calendaring was just a different version of making lists. Out of sight, out of mind. Though, of course, in a different context, calendaring is an excellent tool.

What complicated this whole situation and made it even more frustrating was that I had a strong need for my actions in the world to make spiritual sense. Yes, spiritual sense. There had to be meaning and purpose to my earthly activity that directly related to my soul truth, whatever that was.

The dreams I wanted to fulfill and the things I wanted to create had to have a spiritual basis, not just be desires of my human personality. As I'm sure you know and have probably experienced, desires of the human personality, once fulfilled, simply lead to more desires. It's an endless hunger that always leads to emptiness and meaninglessness. I experienced that early in life and quickly realized that was not the way to happiness and fulfillment.

I also knew from experience and from reading spiritual books that my thoughts create my reality, and more than anything I wanted to consciously utilize this universal principle. I wanted to align my thoughts with spiritual truth. A tall order, you might say. However, I always had a deep inner conviction that there had to be a way to bring these different pieces of spirit and matter into one smooth, organic process of living on earth.

A whole new level of urgency to discover and live in this integrated manner emerged when I started giving psychic readings and psychically saw exactly how our thoughts create our reality.

In sessions with clients I psychically saw, for the first time, the human aura, the human energy field. I saw that, at the core, everything is energy. I saw that thoughts are energy. Emotions are energy. Our history exists in the aura as energy I could psychically read. I saw how, when thoughts gathered, they manifested in physical form as objects and experiences that became our reality.

I also saw our divine aspect. I saw how it was ever present with love and always available for help and guidance. In this part of the aura, the divine part as I call it, I also saw the person's talents, abilities and purpose.

Over the years, from many sessions with clients, this became very clear: For us to experience the greatest fulfillment in life, we need to be aligned with our soul truth and we need to be aligned with universal truth—live and act from that truth and, most of all, consciously create in the world from that deeper truth.

What I learned in these sessions validated my long-held belief that there had to be a more integrated way to live in the world; they also explained my sense of urgency to do so.

Given all this information, it was clear what I was looking for was a way to organize my life that was based on spiritual truths and spiritual principles that easily led to physical action—getting things done that I needed to get done and creating things I wanted to create.

What I needed, without knowing I did, was a visual planning/creating system that took into account the entire spectrum of earth-spirit activity. This visual presentation, a picture of the whole, would make sense of the parts and the whole simultaneously. It would clarify purpose and determine and prioritize earthly activity.

It took some time, but I finally put it all together and it was because of an experience I had when looking to purchase a car.

I had visited many dealerships, test-driven many cars and brought home many brochures. There was one car I was particularly interested in and was seriously considering buying. I placed that brochure, with the picture of the car, where I could always see it. Daily I'd look at the picture of the car and think about whether I should buy it.

After a while, I purchased the car. It turned out to be the worst car I had ever owned for many reasons. It had mechanical problems right away. Working with the dealership was difficult. Most importantly, it was not a safe car to drive. Fortunately, I resolved all those issues fairly quickly. However, the value of that experience was priceless and far-reaching. It was the most important lesson I could have had in manifesting.

The fact that I saw the picture of that car daily is why I ended up buying the car. It was a simple law of manifestation: I focused on it; I got it. It didn't matter whether I really wanted the car or whether it was the best car for me!

That's what thought does. It gathers and creates. Things you want and things you don't want. If there is strong, consistent focus, there is creation. That's how it is most of the time, though not all of the time.

It was the combination of these factors—my experience with the car purchase, knowledge of the spiritual principle that thought creates and my insight into how energy operates—that gave me the idea for the Planning System: A method of planning and creating that takes into account all aspects of reality.

The Planning System is excellent for everyone, especially for creative and spiritual people who tend to think in wholes, who respond visually and who expect to follow intuition when making decisions. It is based on the natural laws of the universe. It is easy and simple to use. Best of all, it is powerful and effective.

If you've struggled to organize your life, as I have, never could quite get a grip, never could quite figure out the direction of your life, the purpose or a way to integrate spirit and matter, get ready for success and fulfillment.

In this book I will show you a method of planning and manifesting that will help you create the things you want, change the life conditions you want to change and get done things you want to get done—and all this in alignment with your divine self, working in harmony with the laws of the universe.

In the next chapter I will share with you what I see in the human energy field. I will show you how energy operates in the field and how it connects to your divine self and God energy. This will make it clear how your thoughts create your reality.

As I've said, we are happiest when we create from our soul truth. In Chapter 2 I will help you distinguish your soul truth from all the other "truths" out there. By letting go of superficial standards and conventions, you will be freed to create from your soul truth.

However, in order to create from your soul truth, you have to be able to hear your inner guidance, hear the promptings of your soul; you have to have a good connection with your divine self. In Chapter 3 I will show you what you can do to strengthen this connection.

By giving psychic readings, I have discovered that many of us are unaware of the extent of our power to create all kinds of things in life. I myself was astounded; I didn't know either. The truth is you can not only create things and fulfill dreams, but also dramatically change entire life conditions. That is what I will talk about in Chapter 4.

Then in Chapter 5 you will make a list of all the things you want to create and all the things you want to get done as the first step in using the Planning System.

In Chapter 6 I will show you the Planning System and how it works. It is easy, as I've already said, and simple; though you will have to take time and give serious thought to what you wish to create, because you will create it.

In Chapter 7 we will implement the Planning System and get you going on getting things done and creating things you want to create.

In Chapter 8 I will address something very important: *Being willing* to receive all the wonderful things in life. Are you surprised? Yes, for some of us the biggest obstacle to having what we want is being unwilling to receive it. At the core of this seeming unwillingness is fear of change, fear of the unknown. Learning how to move into the unknown and get to the other side, is one of the greatest skills one can have in life; it is the portal to your greatest fulfillment. I want to makes sure the fear of change does not stop you from creating what you want.

In Chapter 9 I share with you what stayed at the forefront of my mind as I was writing this book: To encourage you to use the Planning System to change unhappy life conditions. I also share with you some of my own experiences in using the Planning System.

Next in the book is a meditation to inspire you and remind you of your divine nature. Please read it slowly, perhaps with some beautiful music in the background and take in the majesty of your own being. There you will also find a link where you can download the audio version of this powerful guided meditation.

A quick reference guide of the steps you need to take to manifest your desires follows.

At the end of the book is the Supporting Material section. This is an important part of the book. Listed are books, guided meditations and other tools for spiritual development. I encourage you to take advantage of these wonderful resources.

At the end, I have a couple of blank pages where you can record your successful manifestations and a couple of blank pages for notes.

Lastly, I want to ask you to please use information in this book that resonates with you. Ignore information that does not resonate with you. We are all unique and need information that's appropriate for our current needs and that suits our nature. Don't force anything. Always accept only what feels right to you.

Now, let's begin. We will start with a closer look at the human aura, the human energy field so you can see how energy operates in the field and see how your thoughts and beliefs create your reality. The Planning System is based on these universal principles; the more you understand how energy operates, the more successful you will be in using the Planning System to create the things you want to create and get done things you want to get done.

1.

Your Thoughts & Beliefs Create Your Reality

From my doctoral research into quantum physics, I knew that, fundamentally, everything is energy. What I didn't expect is to be able to *see* that energy. Yet, that is exactly what happened in my first official psychic reading session. I was surprised and awed to see that beyond physical manifestation everything is energy.

Across from me sat my first client and I psychically saw her as a map of energy. I saw her current and past events as energy. I saw her divine aspect as energy. These various energies flowed, interacted with each other, influenced each other and connected to the world and people.

Beyond the energy field of my client was the vast field of God energy, or energy of All That Is, or whatever name you like to use for the great divine. We all exist in this vast field of God energy or, more accurately, we are God energy, since there is no outside to this field. In this way, we are all connected, one, an aspect of All That Is. We cannot be anything else or be anywhere else.

In a psychic reading session, I also see the client's thoughts as energy, thoughts from the present and also from any other time in her life. I see them around the head. To me, thoughts look like strings. (To other psychics they may look different.) Very strong thoughts, held over a long period of time, look thicker and darker.

These thoughts and beliefs are the person's identity. So when you look at someone, what you are seeing is a construct of the person's thoughts and beliefs, including the person's history and a number of other elements. This is who this person is, the person you know as Ed or Jenny or Sarah. If she changed the energy in her aura, changed her thoughts and beliefs, she would be another person, look different, feel different, act different, make different life choices and probably have different friends.

The longer a person holds a thought in his mind, the stronger the thought becomes. It becomes a belief. It sets up as the person's permanent identity. The thoughts and beliefs may have been generated at any point in the person's life; they will prevail unless changed either volitionally or by external factors.

Hate, anger, jealousy, resentment, bitterness and the like, are damaging thoughts. If held over a long period of time, they have overall destructive effects, including damage to the body. Their presence automatically blocks divine energies, which automatically provide healing and guidance. More about that in a minute.

Whatever your deepest beliefs, they are you, who you are as a human being. You will act in the world from these beliefs. People will respond to you given this set of beliefs. And that is your reality, your life.

To change your life, you have to change your thoughts, your beliefs. In doing so, you will change your aura. With your aura changed, you are a different person. Being a different person, you will act differently, others will see you differently and respond to you differently and you will create and experience different life situations, a different reality.

Most of us don't know that our thoughts and beliefs create our reality. We may not even be conscious of our thoughts and beliefs. We've lived with them so long they are essentially unconscious. That we have a choice about what to think and what to believe may never have occurred to us. However, once we understand that our thoughts and beliefs create our reality, we can take charge and make adjustments. We can move forward to consciously create our lives.

This is not as difficult or mysterious as it sounds—the process of identifying your thoughts and beliefs. All you have to do is notice where you are not happy. Then examine what you think about the situation; examine what you believe about the situation—yes, these thoughts and beliefs are creating it. Even a quick analysis will instantly yield insight and can begin to improve your situation.

In addition to the person's thoughts, beliefs and history, I also see the person's divine aspect. This is my absolute favorite topic to talk about and certainly my most favorite topic to contemplate.

The divine self is like the most beautiful music you will have ever heard, the kind you might hear in dreams but nowhere in waking life. Your divine self is not somewhere else, far away, it is right here with you, in you, you!—an aspect of you. It is responsive to your every thought, feeling, movement, desire, inclination. It is available for input and guidance. It eagerly awaits your questions and requests. Above all, it absolutely loves to communicate with you. It very much wants a relationship with you. And, most wonderful of all, it is pure love. You are sitting in a warm, protective cocoon of your divine self, ensconced in the love of God.

Remember that when you feel all alone and when you don't know what to do.

Ever since I saw this "arrangement," the way we are our divine self, when I feel lost and alone, I remember what I saw. Peace and comfort descend. Eventually, answers and guidance come.

Now, what can block the experience of the presence of your divine self, as I said earlier, are your own thoughts and beliefs. There can be so many of them occupying so much space, the divine self can't reach you to offer love, comfort and guidance. Or, to say it another way—the divine is always present with love, comfort and guidance. However, when you have many human thoughts, you block the experience of the divine energies.

Given this situation, you can see why it would be important to learn to stay aware of your thoughts. You can understand them to be a part of your human personality and not necessarily any absolute truth. Seeing them this way, you automatically clear the space for the perception of the divine.

It is also easy to see why it would be important to remove any beliefs that say your divine self is far away somewhere and difficult to access. That very belief will stop you from experiencing the divine which is always present.

To say it another way—since we are spirit first, our human expression sustained by spiritual energy, by God energy, our human life depends on spirit. If we cut off from spirit, through our thoughts and beliefs, we suffer.

Especially damaging, as I said earlier, is the presence of an abundance of destructive thoughts. In that situation the body cannot receive the benefits of spirit. It cannot receive continuous healing that naturally happens when we are in alignment with universal qualities of joy, love, peace, beauty and the like.

We all vibrate God energies to different degrees. We are all learning and growing. The goal is to consciously align and work in partnership with the divine. Soul expressing in matter consciously is the goal of human evolution. We're striving to be the divine humans that in truth we are—here on earth.

One of the ways we grow here on earth is by fulfilling our life purpose. In psychic reading sessions I see the client's talents, gifts and abilities and also her soul purpose. What I see is that the person is happiest when she is using her authentic abilities and on track with fulfilling her soul purpose. This also happens to be the easiest path.

We have free will, so it is up to us to choose ways to express our talents and abilities. In other words, the vehicle or the form for the expression of our talents and abilities is ours to choose. There are many forms and many vehicles. We choose the one we like best.

Overall, ideally, you are attuned to your divine self. You ask for and accept guidance. You move and create in the world from divine guidance and inspiration. You grow, expand in consciousness, evolve as a human being and as soul and are fulfilled as a human being and as soul. And, ideally, when you work with the Planning System, you will keep all this in mind as a way to create effectively and what is for your highest good.

To clear the path to your inner guidance and become aware of what you want to create that has deep value and is in support of your life purpose, it is important to be conscious of influences that make it difficult to hear your soul self. Societal and family expectations play a big part in our ability to know and follow our authentic path. Given these influences, how do you recognize the voice of your soul? How do you untangle family and societal expectations from your deepest truth? How do you tell apart your soul voice from the voice of your human personality? That is what I will talk about next.

2.

You Are Happiest When You Create from Your Soul Truth

For you to use the Planning System in a way that is most effective and brings greatest fulfillment, it is best that you create from soul truth. But how do you tell apart soul truth from all the "truths" that are out there in the world?

In this chapter we will identify the most prevalent "truths" and separate them from spiritual truth. That way you can let go of everything that is not your deepest truth, hear your own inner voice and let it lead you to create that which is of highest benefit to your being, which is also always of highest benefit to everyone else.

We all grow up in a society. Every society on the planet has its own beliefs, values and conventions. If you examine the values and conventions of the many social groups and societies that have existed on earth throughout millennia, you will be amazed to discover the diversity—one of those conventions being the sacrifice of human beings as a way to please the gods for one reason or another.

When we are born, we are born at a specific time in history, in a society that holds certain beliefs, values and conventions. It is important to understand that these standards happen to be "truth" at that particular time in history and in that particular location on the planet. They may not be truth at another time in history or at another location on the planet.

Furthermore, just because a society holds certain values does not mean that those values are either "right" or any kind of ultimate truth. Additionally, societies in general, do not necessarily reflect spiritual truths. And they certainly do not necessarily support an individual's spiritual growth and unique journey on planet earth.

By giving psychic readings, I have seen just how unique we are and how unique our life purposes and life journeys. Many of my clients have suffered because their lives did not match the current society's expectations of what a successful life should look like—and there is no need for that suffering if you understand the relatively arbitrary nature of standards and conventions.

So, here you are on planet earth at this time in history in a society that happens to hold certain standards of how life should be lived and how you should be as a human being—and that may have absolutely nothing to do with who you really are as a soul or what your own individual life purpose may be.

What do you do? How do you tell the two apart? After all, you grew up with these beliefs. You didn't have a choice. You may have accepted societal values as ultimate truth. You may have tried to live up to these expectations. You may also have felt the dissonance: You were doing the "right" things and feeling all wrong doing them. I empathize. This can be very painful and confusing.

Worse yet, you may have grown up in a family which strictly upheld societal standards. Then you were not only beaten up by society in general but by your own family, if you did not adhere to prescribed standards of "appropriateness" as a human being.

It is almost impossible to find your life path with this kind of pressure and indoctrination. Yet, hearing your own inner voice and following your own inner guidance is the only way to peace and fulfillment in life. What a dilemma! No wonder so many of us are lost, unhappy, confused and continually searching.

Let's get one thing straight. Societal standards are not necessarily spiritual standards. Your obligation is to follow your deepest soul truth. Your challenge is to find a way to do this in the society in which you are born. This can be done and is being done, even if difficult, but only if you know that the standards of society are arbitrary for this time and place in history, not any ultimate truth.

As I've said, sitting in sessions with clients over the years, I have seen just how different we are as human beings and just how different our purposes are. I have freed many clients from the burden of societal expectations and released them into the freedom of their own soul truth and their own life path. When you are free to pursue your truth, you then start to make choices that have deep meaning and value for you and that offer deep fulfillment.

Ideally, you will be using the Planning System to actualize your deepest truth. But first you have to know what your truth is.

Here, today, we will take the time to separate spiritual truth from the values of our current Western society. We will liberate you from societal expectations and release you into that vast territory of your soul truth, power and potential.

A Partial List of Our Current Social Values & Expectations & Spiritual Truth

You Have to Have a Lot of Money and a Lot of Things to Have Value as a Human Being

There are some people whose life purpose is to use their soul power to create many things on the physical plane and, as a result, create a lot of wealth. This is a big chal-

lenge—to create in the physical. Additionally, there is the important challenge of how the person handles that wealth and who he becomes with all that wealth. These are legitimate soul challenges and grow the individual and the soul in important ways.

However, that's certainly not everybody's life purpose.

The very opposite I've seen of this particular life purpose is a very personal journey where the individual's growth is internal. No one can see that activity. There is no evidence of this work being done in the physical. The person can easily be judged for lack of apparent productivity. Yet, nothing could be further from the truth.

The path for this person is to be here on earth and work out within himself meaning and purpose; it has nothing to do with creating lots of things in the physical world. In fact, the soul may have purposely chosen to withhold wealth for this lifetime as a way to assure a laser focus on spiritual development.

For this person, this life may also not be about having extensive relationships with other people or a specific romantic involvement. It is a solo journey, all the work happening inside, privately, invisible to others.

In our society today, where what job you have and what possessions you have is the standard of success, the challenge becomes to establish within your own being a deep sense of self-worth, even as you live in a society that holds these other values of success. That is part of your challenge and part of your growth and evolution.

Bottom line: Your value as a human being does not depend on fulfilling current social expectations. You don't have to run around doing and creating all the things society expects you to do and create, an important fact to remember when you start working with the Planning System.

The spiritual truth is this: You are an aspect of God. Your value is intrinsic. You cannot not have value. Just as you are, you are important, valuable and, above all, always loved and accepted wholly, completely and unconditionally by your Creator. This is true for you as a personality, as a human being, and it is also true for you as an individual soul.

You have value, you are acceptable, you are treasured just because you exist. Being an aspect of God, an expression of God, it cannot be any other way. Sit with that a while and let it go deep into your being. Breathe.

You Have to Have Children
No you don't. It is not everyone's life purpose to experience growth, expansion and fulfillment through a family dynamic. If you do not feel deep within your being the desire to have children, don't let yourself be talked into it.

From a spiritual perspective, over lifetimes we incarnate with many of the same souls creating family groups but playing different roles in the family. Many times children are had as a way to make future incarnations possible for the soul. If you are not coming back to this earth plane, you will not need physical bodies into which to incarnate.

So, if you've been pushed to have children when you really don't want to have them, feel free to completely let go of that idea and move on with your life in the direction you feel the calling, the inspiration, the excitement.

All the Other Things You're Supposed to Do, Be & Want

This list is endless. Your success and self-worth depend on these things: You're supposed to own certain things; like certain things; enjoy certain events; behave a certain way; look a certain way; wear certain clothes; have a certain kind of wedding—the list goes on and on.

If you have to do all these things to feel you have value, you will end up doing all sorts of things you may not really want to do, try to like all sorts of things you don't really like and, in the end, feel . . . miserable, empty and unfulfilled.

Worst of all, trying to do all this will confuse you; you want and feel one thing, but you're told you're supposed to want and feel something else because that something else is the right thing to want and the right way to feel.

Make the effort to identify the social "rights" that

don't feel true to you and let them go. Start to pay closer attention to that voice deep inside you that tells you what is right for you and do that instead.

No longer allow the value of yourself to depend on any external factor.

You Have This Idea That Your Life Purpose Has to Be Something Grand & Glitzy, Something Very Specific & Easily Identifiable. You've Not Found It & You're Miserable.

This is simply not true and, worse yet, this belief can take you away from your soul truth. Not in touch with your soul truth, you can't create a life that satisfies you.

In my experience, there has been a lot of value to the New Age movement, but also a lot of damage has been done.

Let's be honest. New Age thought is just another belief system, like any other. It's human made. It is not ultimate truth. This belief system is interpreted by people as everything else is interpreted by people. People will understand the concepts and apply them as they understand them—and sometimes to their own detriment—as all belief systems have been applied throughout human history all over the world.

Ultimately, one finds and experiences spiritual truth within one's own being. As J. Krishnamurti said, "Truth is a pathless land, and you cannot approach it by any path whatsoever, by any religion, by any sect." It's a personal, inner journey.

One area where I have seen New Age thought bring a lot of suffering is around the idea of life purpose.

Many people interpret the notion of life purpose to mean something one can easily and quickly discover by taking a weekend workshop. That is not how it is most of the time.

Although a workshop can facilitate a deeper understanding of one's self, it may not necessarily yield an absolute answer as to what one's life purpose may be. So, don't be frustrated if you've taken these workshops without the results you were seeking.

What is true is that, most of the time, one automatically comes to live one's life purpose by simply living and following one's own built-in impulses.

If you are under the influence of New Age thinking that says you will find your life purpose somewhere and are focused on looking for it—stop.

This is the situation. While you are focused on trying to find your life purpose somewhere, you are missing signals from your soul that will get you there. Let go of the idea of "finding" your life purpose and focus on listening to your inner promptings.

When you are born, built into you are desires and interests, impulses directing you toward certain actions and activities. They are meant to guide you in life. They are meant to propel you to actualize your life purpose. As you can see, paying attention to those soul impulses and following through on them is critical. I will talk more about hearing your inner promptings and connecting with your divine self in the next chapter.

Now I will share with you the different life purposes I have seen with my clients in psychic reading sessions.

As hard as it might be to accept, for most people a life purpose is something very simple from the perspective of our human eyes but very important from the eyes of the soul. So if you are focused on searching for that glitzy life purpose—stop. Focus on your deepest desires and longings. They will lead you to your fullest self-expression and satisfaction.

A Partial List of What a Life Purpose Can Be

- To experience a large variety of life situations, including many types of work and many kinds of people. This puts you in many challenging life situations ideal for growth and expansion in consciousness.
- You have a family and within the family dynamic you grow, learn, evolve and experience fulfillment.
- You are a luminous soul. You are here simply to be a light. That's it. It's up to you to choose any job or career you like that feels most fun to you. As a light, you bring in the energy, the frequency of light. The presence of that frequency raises consciousness in everyone around you. In that higher frequency, they are connected to their own

light and make better choices and make the world a better place. All in all, you are here to raise consciousness on the planet by facilitating higher consciousness everywhere you go.

- As mentioned earlier, you can be here for an internal, solo journey. You are alone to work out and synthesize spirit and matter, to experience consciously being in the body while being spirit.
- You are here for a very specific reason. Every client who I have seen who has come here on a mission, to do something very specific, meant she was not going to do other things in life. She was not necessarily going to have a life partner or family or do some other things most people do. Or she was to meet her life partner much later in life and this partner would be a partner in her mission. Usually these folks are here to introduce new consciousness, new innovations, to change the shape and structure of society. In all instances these people have an exceptional ability to focus. They have tremendous power and excellent organizing and people skills.

If this sounds like you, you no longer need to be frustrated with social expectations—the timing of when you should get married, have children and so on. Instead, get excited; you are here to not only do some important work but also to experience tremendous success and satisfaction.

- You are an artist and you are here to bring in new consciousness through your art.

I have seen many artists for psychic readings. I have to say, they are wonderful to look at psychically. In the artist the crown chakra is open. Artists are naturally connected to spirit. They receive visions and inspiration from the spirit world. Their job is to bring those visions into the physical—without a doubt a challenging journey for many reasons, one of them the perpetual journey into the unknown as a way to bring their art into the world. I will talk more about that later. Through the vehicle of their art, whichever form it takes, artists bring fresh perspectives, novel possibilities and new consciousness to the planet.

If you are an artist, look to your inner self for guidance as to the steps you need to take to bring your art into the world. Accept and learn from your challenges. You are here to do important work. Your art has value. You have value. Carry on!

These are just a few examples of what a life purpose may look like amidst tremendous variety.

Knowledge of one's life purpose may not be something one just knows instantly, as I've been saying, though some people know this early on. More often than not, one lives life listening to inner promptings, following interests, exploring curiosities, learning from present experiences and so on. With these life experiences, one attains a variety of life skills, learns how to deal with people, basically learns how to operate in society, learns how to operate in the physical dimension. Eventually, a focus starts to emerge that, in time, becomes the expression of one's life purpose, and all those skills and knowledge acquired over the years, are brought together and applied to this purpose. All in all, those initial explorations will automatically lead to what the person loves to do and some work that utilizes the person's natural gifts and abilities. That, in turn, leads to success and fulfillment.

There are exceptions to this path. For example, if one is on a solo journey of focused spiritual development. The journey continues to be an internal one. The same is true for the soul who is here to experience many different life situations as a way to develop. These journeys do not necessarily culminate in a specific external expression. Instead, the journey may culminate in simply *being*—the embodiment of joy, love, peace, greater wisdom. The person becomes a beacon of light and in this way raises consciousness in the world. I bring this up to make sure that those of you who are on these kinds of journeys let go of trying to finally arrive at some destination that looks like what society expects or what your friends have.

I remember having one client who was frustrated that his life didn't look like that of his friends. He moved a lot, changed jobs often and had no life partner. He wondered what was wrong with him. His friends were "settled," why wasn't he?

Well, there was nothing wrong with him. His purpose on earth was to do exactly what he was doing, have as many different life experiences as possible. Settling down in one place with one job and one relationship wasn't his path. I wish you could have seen his face when I told him about his life purpose. All the strain and anguish instantly drained from it. He became luminous. Truth does that; it sets you free.

As you can see, souls incarnate for dramatically different reasons. If you have tried to live up to your family's expectations or social expectations and have been unsuccessful, it may be that your reason for being here is very different from those expectations. Breathe a nice deep breath of relief, start listening to those inner promptings you've been forced to ignore because you were so focused on fulfilling family and social expectations and get excited about living your own unique life.

Your Only Option for Healing Is to See a Medical Doctor

Many people believe that is their only option, to see a medical doctor, when they are ill, that their well-being rests on his or her authority. This is the culture in which we are born but it isn't ultimate truth.

I know alternative ways of healing are continuing to gain in popularity, however, we have a ways to go. To that end, I believe it is very important to understand modern medicine in the context of the history of healing.

Very early humans operated from instinct. When they fell ill, they collected herbs and used them to treat themselves. They didn't go and see a healer. No such healer existed. Instead, they healed themselves.

Later on in history, when there were official healers, shamans, medicine men and the like, illness and healing were viewed wholistically. Disease was not seen as only of the body but also of the spirit. Healers interceded to affect a change in the person's consciousness as a way to heal the body.

In ancient Greece there were healing temples to which the sick traveled to heal. There they talked to priests who were also healers. The two functions were not separate. The body and the soul were addressed as one as a way to heal. The patients were guided by priest healers to seek within themselves the cause of their illness and also the cure. They were given private rooms where they requested from their soul self to be given a dream that explained the cause of their illness. With that knowledge, healing was initiated.

Early physicians, that evolved into our present-day physicians, started off healing the body along with prayer and other non-physical remedies. Over the centuries, the focus narrowed down to the treatment of the body only.

Today, the modern physician sees illness as an occurrence in the body, unrelated to other causal forces, and to be treated in the body only.

So, you see, healing as it is practiced today in our Western world is a small period of time in earth history, a small example of how disease and healing were understood throughout millennia. Today's practices are not ultimate truth. The truth is bigger than the beliefs of the current medical community.

My own understanding of what it means to be well and what it means to be ill has deepened since I started giving psychic readings. In sessions with clients, I see how thoughts and beliefs impact the body, as I've talked about in the last chapter. If thoughts and beliefs create reality, they also create the reality of the body. If your body is ailing, almost always, the healing has to happen in consciousness first, in thought and belief, and then the healing in the body will follow. This is a process of coming back into alignment with your soul truth. The human personality can interfere with soul truth through thoughts and beliefs. However, one can change one's thoughts and beliefs and come back into alignment with one's soul truth and come back to health.

So, if you are looking to heal physically and one of your intentions for the Planning System is to initiate that healing, think in these larger terms of what healing is, what wellness is. That way you can set into motion fundamental forces to achieve alignment with your soul truth and regain optimal well-being.

All in all, for you to use the Planning System to create that which most fulfills you, you need to create from soul truth. To create from soul truth, you have to be able to hear the voice of your soul, your authentic self. And in order to hear your soul self, you may need to let go of some current social norms and conventions that are acting like static, making it hard for you to hear your soul truth.

Before you move on to the next chapter, it might be a good idea to reflect on what social norms you have accepted that are just that: Social norms active at this time in history. See which ones never rang true for you and which you are happily ready to let go so you can create room for what you really value, room for your soul truth.

Are there any other "truths" that have come to mind, when you read this chapter, that you realize are not your deepest truth and which you are ready to let go?

Also, think back on those times when you have heard your soul speaking to you and acted on its suggestion and those times you heard it and did not act on its suggestion. Consider setting the intention to pay closer attention to hear the guidance and make a decision to follow through on the guidance.

If you would like to better hear the voice of your divine

self, feel its promptings; if you would like to use the Planning System to create from this deeper part of your being, then turn the page and I will show you what you can do to strengthen this connection.

3.

Establish a Strong Connection with Your Divine Self

You have to have a good, clear connection to your divine self in order to hear guidance and create from this deeper part of your being.

All of us receive communication from our divine self. I am sure if you stopped and thought about it, you can recall such times in your life. Most of the time, though, we are simply unaware of that voice. This is something like being so preoccupied that you don't hear someone call your name.

There are many ways to establish a clear connection with your soul self. Here I will show you a few ways to begin to establish this communication. My suggestions are based on what I have learned from giving psychic readings about how energy operates in the human aura and how transformation happens.

Let's begin by remembering two very important facts.

First, your divine self *is you*. It is another aspect of you. It is the part of you that is close to God. Your human personality, on the other hand, is close to earth; it needs to be so that it can successfully operate in the physical world.

Second, your divine self is here with you, right now. It is not somewhere else far away. You don't have to travel a long, hard journey to get to it.

With this in mind, it's easy to see that all it takes to communicate with this deeper part of you is the decision to do so. What is key is *intention*. Your clear intention, your strong decision to communicate with your divine self, sets powerful forces in motion.

The reason intention is so important is because behind your intention is the belief that communication with your divine self is possible and can be accomplished. You *believe* you can communicate with your divine aspect. And, as all beliefs work, you will begin the process of establishing a relationship with this deeper part of your being.

If you would like to begin to have a deep connection with your divine self and want to start right now, here are some things you can do to begin the process.

Journal About Your Desire to Have A Relationship with Your Divine Self

As a way to begin to focus the mind and initiate creation, you first have to clear any doubts, fears, anxieties, hesitations, trepidations and concerns you may have about being able to create what you want. All concerns and hesitations get in the way of a laser focus—which is what you need in order to create anything.

A good way to clear fears and worries is to journal. Of course, you can also always talk to someone as a way to neutralize opposing energies.

As you journal, consider: How do you feel about having a deeper connection with your divine self? What would that look like? What would it feel like? Are you afraid? Are you excited? Do you have any doubts about having this connection? What worries you most about having this connection? What do you expect from this connection? How would your life be different if you had this connection? How might you be different?

As you consider these questions, pay close attention to what happens in your body. Do you feel a tightening in your belly? Stop and see what that is about—fear, anxiety, excitement? Journal about that. Do you feel any tension in your neck, shoulders, legs, or any other part of your body? Stop and explore that. What is the tension about? Are you holding your breath? Relax and begin to breathe normally. Find out why you were holding your breath.

Our body has comprehensive information as to how we *really* feel about everything—as opposed to how we *think* we feel, how we think we *should* feel and what we *allow* ourselves to feel.

Feelings come from thoughts—even if those thoughts are unconscious. So if you pay attention to your body and notice the sensations and feelings, you can begin to know your unconscious thoughts—the ones that create your reality.

Through this journaling exploration you make conscious any obstacles, in the form of beliefs and feelings, that may interfere with your intention to create what you want. Being conscious of the obstacles, you begin to dissolve them.

Make a Formal Declaration

By giving psychic readings I have discovered that a formal declaration is necessary to initiate any creating project.

Thinking and ruminating about creating something and actually making a decision to create it are two very different energy states. This is the way they look in the aura.

When you "think" you want something and you're considering it, mulling it over, on the fence about it, the aura is filled with a mixture of thoughts and feelings—fear, anxiety, doubt, excitement, worry, curiosity, hope, exhilaration and so on; lots of contradictory, opposing energies—none of them very powerful.

It takes a unified energy to create something. A laser focus. That gives it power.

All those vague, contradicting energies in the aura have to be cleared before manifestation can happen. A sharp focus needs to be created.

You create a sharp focus by sitting down and addressing all your concerns through journaling, talking to someone, listening to a guided meditation and so on, as I've already said.

When all the concerns have been addressed and there are no niggling doubts left, you should feel a clarity of direction, a strong conviction, a powerful determination. All of you is absolutely positive you want to create something. There is no doubt. When you are in this state, all the forces are united in the chosen direction. Your thoughts will have moved away from worry and hesitation and are now engaged in moving forward, focused on how you can create what you want.

In the aura, the contradicting thoughts and feelings will have receded. In their place are new thoughts and feelings about the direction in which you are heading.

So, when you feel ready, after you've journaled and done what you need to do to clear fears and doubts and you feel you're ready, pick a time and formally declare your decision to set up this relationship with your divine self.

Once you have formally declared your intention, you then begin to take steps to establish a strong connection with your divine self.

Work with Guided Meditations to Help You Connect with Your Divine Self

I consider guided meditations a modality of transformation in its own right. With guided meditations you can: Uncover unconscious obstacles to your manifestation project; train yourself—through the use of your imagination—to get used to the new conditions you want to create; powerfully introduce whole new states of consciousness as a way to advance moving into a higher vibration of being; relax and realign with your divine self; receive answers and guidance from your divine self; receive universal wisdom; heal childhood patterns and much more.

It is an easy modality to use. It does not take much time. It rarely costs much to purchase a guided meditation, yet it offers so much. I wish more people would take advantage of this simple, yet powerful tool of transformation.

At the end of the book, in the Supporting Materials section, I have a list of guided meditations to help you with many aspects of your life. Most of them are free. Use them to help you connect with your divine self. With sustained focus, you can make tremendous leaps in your spiritual development.

Work with Your Dreams as A Way to Establish a Strong Connection with Your Divine Self

Ever since I can remember, I felt the presence of the divine in waking life and in the dream state. In dreams I received insight, answers, guidance, warnings and precognitions. Most importantly, I received comfort. I was not alone in this world. I felt a distinct, unquestionable sense that there is a deeper world that is more powerful that is sustaining me.

If you're not already working with your dreams, I recommend you start. In working with your dreams, you will be able to receive continuous assurance, comfort and support from your deeper being. Your daily life and your dreaming life will be a united whole. When you go to sleep at night, you will not be blanking out, but entering a world where you will receive help, insight and comfort and be in communion with your soul and All That Is.

So, before you go to bed at night, tell your divine self you would like to experience its presence and are open to receive its guidance.

How do you do that?

You keep in mind that your inner self, your soul self, is you, a deeper part of you. It's right there with you. It's always listening. Then you talk to it and tell it what you would like. It's that simple.

Nothing may happen at first. However, if you continue to make the request, something will happen. One way or another, you will hear from your divine self.

When I seek an urgent answer from my dreams, I don't usually receive it the night I make the request, but a night or two later. And then the answer is crystal clear. I wake up with everything changed around the situation for which I requested help and insight.

Dreams and dream symbols are highly individual. Once you start working with your dreams, you will discover your own dream patterns and symbols.

A Quiet Mind Is Needed

It's easiest to hear your divine self when your mind is quiet. If your mind is busy, the messages from your divine self will come, but you won't be able to notice them because your attention is elsewhere.

Once you make the decision to hear your inner guidance, it would be good to make yourself available to hear it.

You might decide, if you are not doing so already, to begin to meditate daily as a way to slow down and enter deep silence and stillness.

If you don't want to do a formal meditation, just sit and breathe and be. Rest your mind. Take it away from the preoccupation with earthly things. Allow yourself to experience yourself in the larger Reality.

You can also listen to some beautiful music or a guided meditation to take a break from physical reality and enter and rest in the spiritual realm.

What I've been doing for a long time is, what I call, communion. I take my attention away from earthly things and shift it to the divine realms. The divine realms are joy, love, peace, beauty, harmony—the eternal conditions of God energy. In this way, I rest and re-energize and my perspective and priorities recalibrate.

The quieter you are, the more still your mind and being, the easier it will be to hear your inner self.

Regularly entering deep stillness, your connection to the divine can yield amazing results. You might be able to receive unprecedented insight and information. Ultimately, all the knowledge of the universe becomes accessible to you. To say that this is a most wonderful place to be in your spiritual development is an understatement. It's pure freedom, peace and power.

In addition to these suggestions, as to how to establish a strong connection with your divine self, there are many other things you can do. You can read spiritual books; join spiritual groups; go on silent retreats; join a meditation group; attend spiritual conferences; watch talks and interviews with spiritual teachers and so on. Basically, the more spiritual work you do, the stronger your connection will become. Just make sure you don't force yourself into anything that does not feel right.

If establishing a strong connection with your divine self becomes your manifestation project, you can explore additional ways to support yourself in establishing this connection.

What Does Guidance from the Divine Self Feel Like?

Once you make a decision to establish this communication, begin to pay attention to the presence of your divine self and to its promptings. These become especially noticeable when you are making decisions.

This is what your inner promptings, your soul impulses may feel like: You are deeply curious about something and want to explore; you really want to learn how to do something, like knitting or ballroom dancing or singing; you love something deeply and want to pursue it even though it does not make logical sense; you feel called to just sit and do nothing; you have a strong sense to call someone; you very badly want to travel somewhere; you keep getting nudges from the inside to go somewhere, maybe to a bookstore, all across town—for no apparent reason.

Soul impulses tend to feel a bit unusual, a bit different from what normally passes through your mind. The voice of your soul does not scream at you. There is no nervous urgency. It's a gentle voice with a suggestion. If the message is important, it will come back again and again. In situations when your life is in danger, the voice is very loud and very clear.

If you have asked your divine self for guidance and are waiting for answers, the answers are likely to come when your mind is quiet, as I mentioned earlier. You may be sitting in a waiting room somewhere, your mind on idle or driving for many hours or knitting or waiting at a street light or vacuuming and then, seemingly out of nowhere, the answer just appears in your mind.

Once you start to notice the voice of your divine self, keep paying attention and see how the entire communication process takes place. Examine closely as to what happens from the moment you make your request to the time you receive the answer. This process is unique for all of us. Once you know the pattern, fine tune it, make it work even better.

Of course, when you hear the guidance, follow it. Sometimes you'll see the reason for the guidance right away. Sometimes the guidance will make sense decades later. At that time, you will be glad you followed it. This is especially true when it comes to developing skills and abilities. That art class you really wanted to take but hesitated thinking it frivolous, a waste of time and money, but took anyway, years later came in handy. You found yourself building a website and all those principles of design you learned in that "self-indulgent" art class suddenly became invaluable.

I especially highly recommend following promptings where there is a strong heart desire to learn something, travel somewhere, live somewhere—even if they don't seem to make much sense, aren't practical or seem self-indulgent.

These are the sort of inner nudges whose reason becomes clear much later in life. They are very important for the person's development and life purpose.

Caution—Don't Confuse Soul Impulses with Impulses of the Personality

One caution here about following soul impulses. You may confuse them with the impulses of your personality, your ego self.

Let's make the distinction. Soul impulses are never destructive. Soul promptings are never about you doing something to hurt yourself or someone else. They are never about a compulsive desire to possess some material thing or to possess someone. They never have that insatiable hunger, urgency, nervousness that can accompany the desires of the personality.

However, if your soul is nudging you toward your purpose and you are not getting the message or are unwilling to act on it, you will feel a disquiet, a restlessness. A perfect example of this kind of disquiet is Helen Schucman's experience with the channeling of *A Course in Miracles*.

Dr. Schucman was a clinical psychologist at Columbia University in the 1960s. When it came to her to channel *A Course in Miracles*, she strongly resisted. She wanted nothing to do with the airy-fairy spirituality of channeling. So, at regular intervals, she'd abandon the whole project. The results were always the same. She was restless. She could not sleep. She was unhappy—all up until she picked up the project again and started taking down the message.

It takes quite a bit of spiritual development and concerted effort to hear clearly the guidance of your soul. I suggest you go slowly and carefully. With time you will be able to accurately tell apart the voice of your personality from the voice of your soul.

I encourage you to make the effort to learn to hear your soul guidance. It will give you peace and it will help you to use the Planning System in a way that best supports your whole being and the lives of all beings.

In the next chapter I will talk about the many things that you can create. As I said earlier, you can create so much more than you might have believed possible. I want to make sure you fully understand the power you have in your life. That way you will feel the wonderful freedom to create and change and become—to be the creative being that you really are, express the fundamental quality of All That Is: Creativity—and thereby be a co-creator with the Creator, as you were always meant to be. Let's go.

4.

What Kinds of Things Can You Manifest?

What kinds of things can you create? All kinds of things! Look around:

Are you lacking something in your life—what is it?

Do you yearn for something—for what?

Are you unhappy about something—what would you like instead?

Is there a life condition you would like to improve—what is the better condition?

Is there a quality, such as love or peace, you would like to bring into your life?

Your answers to these questions can be your manifestation projects and you can use the Planning System to make them a reality.

You can create anything—material things, experiences, life conditions, qualities.

All of your life challenges can be your manifestation projects! You don't have to tolerate difficult situations with hopelessness and powerlessness; instead, you can approach them as manifestation projects, as opportunities to create what you want.

As you can see, you can use the Planning System to organize yourself and bring into your life all kinds of wonderful things. Isn't that exciting?!

We are always creating: Ourselves, our lives, our reality—through our thoughts and beliefs—whether or not we are aware of doing so, whether we do it consciously or unconsciously. If we know we are creating our reality, we can choose what reality we want to create. You can use the Planning System to consciously create your life.

Converting Life's Challenges into Manifestation Projects

Perhaps the most important area of your life to which you can apply the Planning System is to solve life's problems.

All of us face challenges daily—painful relationships, problems at work, health issues, financial difficulties or something else. As painful and difficult as these problems may be, ultimately, their purpose is to grow us, evolve us to higher consciousness—to be more God-like. Through challenges we grow and fulfill our life purpose. Therefore, facing challenges and solving problems constructively is possibly the most important activity in life. Often, though, we make this process more difficult than it needs to be.

We are inclined to spend too much time churning our problems instead of moving toward solutions. We worry, are anxious, afraid. In our distress we talk to our friends repeating the same story again and again. We spend time in disbelief about how awful it is. We keep saying, "I just don't know what to do." We do all sorts of things that keep us focused on the problem and in that way we remain stuck, caught, trapped.

Yet, focusing on the problem does not give us solutions. So, what do you do? How do you get out of this mess? Yes, there is a quick way to begin to move out of painful situations. This is what you do.

You ask yourself: What do I want in this situation?

By answering this question, you stop focusing on the problem and begin to focus on the solution. You stop investing your energy and attention on rejecting something you don't want and start directing your energy and attention toward something you do want.

Once you know what you want, you can create it. For example, in the case of a difficult relationship, if you asked yourself what you really wanted, your answer might be peace and harmony.

Let's say the work challenge is that you simply do not like what you are doing. In answer to the question of what you want, the answer might be, work I love.

With a health issue, your answer might be exuberant well-being.

With money difficulties, your answer might be financial peace of mind.

If you face challenges head-on, ask yourself what you want in this situation, then make your answer a manifestation project and use the Planning System to create it, you can then, in this manner, continually create your life—the life you want. And this is pretty darn fantastic!

What Do You *Really* Want?

Let's look more closely at what your desires are really about.

At the deepest level, all desires are a search for God. At the core, all desires are desires for conditions of being, qualities and conditions of God: Joy, love, peace, truth, beauty, creativity, security, safety and the like.

Our desires reflect our natural, organic impulse and aspiration to live divine truth because, in our essence, that is what we are. Instinctively we all know what it's like to be with God. And we continually seek to be there—with our Creator.

In the physical world we express this desire by wanting things that will produce these same feelings, these God qualities. We believe it is things we want, when what we really want are conditions of being, God qualities. It is good not to confuse the two.

For example, many times we seek to create something, let's say money, when what we are really looking for are conditions of being, states of consciousness: Safety, security, prosperity and so on. These are all higher energy states. If we were to attain those higher states of consciousness, money would automatically come.

Reflect on this and possibly, instead of having money as your main manifestation project, though certainly you may also want to have that, the better manifestation project might be to create states of consciousness that will automatically create money, love, peace, trust, safety, security, abundance and so on.

Or, let's say your romantic relationships have not been satisfying, so rather than keep looking for the right person, make it your intention to have qualities and conditions of love and harmony in your life, to be able to receive love.

Or perhaps you might have been sick a lot of your life and your approach has been to deal with each illness one at a time. In this situation, instead of setting the intention to get well from a particular illness, the better intention for your manifesting project might be to establish a condition of permanent exuberant health, well-being and pleasure.

It may be things in your life are not working out in general. To you, it seems you make one bad decision after another. Instead of blaming yourself for your bad decisions and trying to fix the situation one piece at a time, set the intention to live your soul truth, to open to receive love and fulfillment.

So, before you start using the Planning System, reflect deeply on what you *really* want. Are you looking to manifest this object, or are you really looking to live in a certain state of consciousness, or perhaps both? Creating states of consciousness will automatically bring in the object.

Creating Within Smaller Segments of Time

In addition to creating larger projects, you can fine-tune your life by having intentions that address smaller segments of time or smaller manifestations, as Abraham suggests in the channelings by Esther Hicks.

For example, you can have intentions for: A day filled with joy and satisfaction; harmonious interactions with all people you meet during the day; a pleasant visit with your family and so on.

With these intentions you create a certain state of consciousness. Since your thoughts create your reality, by setting positive states of consciousness when stepping into the world, others will see you differently. Perceiving you in this positive state, they will respond by bringing forth their best. In this way you create optimal experiences for all parties involved.

If you make the effort to regularly set intentions for smaller pieces and activities in your life, over time you will set a fundamental positive approach to life.

So, as you can see, you can create much more than just material things. You can create entire life conditions, entire new states of being and consciousness.

Okay, we are ready to move on, but before we do, think about your life.

What would you like to improve, in general? Are there any new life conditions you would like to create? Are there any new qualities you would like to bring into your life? Is there anything rubbing you the wrong way, something painful you've simply accepted and believed impossible to change and improve? Is there a way you would like to step out your door and into the world that would bring positive energy to yourself and to everyone else? If you can, work through to the answers to these questions. That will make the next chapter more fruitful.

When you are ready, proceed to the next chapter. There you will make a list of all the things you want to create and all the tasks you would like to complete. We will use these lists a little later to implement the Planning System.

5.

What Would You Like to Manifest? Let's Start Planning!

It's time to start planning what you would like to manifest and what tasks you would like to complete.

We'll begin by making a couple of lists.

On List One you will write everything you would like to create, the bigger dreams and projects.

On List Two you will write all the things you need to get done for basic living.

Get some paper and a pencil or pen and let's get started. If it works for you, put on some heart-opening music. For me, soft, beautiful music feels like loving arms holding me and makes it easier for me to feel my deepest truth. Maybe it will help you as well. You can try it and see how you feel.

A note about making lists. For linear folks, a piece of paper and a list running down the length of the paper usually works just fine. For visual and creative people, a mind map may work better. How does that work?

You take a piece of paper. A big piece of paper is good, legal size or so. Or, if you like, get an even bigger piece, like newsprint—the paper artists use to draw with pencil and charcoal.

In the middle of the paper write the name of your project. For List One, in the middle of the paper, you might write, My Dreams & Desires. Then all around that central heading you would write all your dreams and desires.

For List Two, in the middle of the paper you might write, All I Have to Get Done. Then all around that central heading, you would write everything you want to get done.

I think mind maps are a spiritual miracle. At a glance, you can see the whole picture. This birds-eye-view brings insight and inspiration and facilitates new ideas; priorities become obvious; next steps become clear.

If you've not planned in this fashion, I highly recommend you try.

All right, let's make our lists.

List One—All I Would Like to Create

On a piece of paper, in the mind map format, if that feels good to you, write down all the things you want to have and all the things you would like to experience; this includes material things as well as qualities and conditions of being.

If in the last chapter you've identified troubling spots and have converted them into wants—something better you would like to create—those desires would go on this list.

Be comprehensive in compiling this list. Any dream you might ever have had goes on this list. Don't hold back. Sometimes we keep secret our deepest desires—even from ourselves. We are afraid our dreams are unreasonable, unachievable, impractical, silly, ridiculous, embarrassing, too expensive and so forth. We worry what others might think.

Remember, to feel fulfilled, healthy and happy, you need to live your soul truth. So don't be afraid to list everything you truly desire from that place deep inside you. No one need see the list. Be brave. This is a good time to start walking your own path in life.

Here are a few examples of things you might have on this list:

Buy a house
Buy a car

Learn to play an instrument
Go to Africa on a safari
Go to Machu Picchu
Work in another country for a year
Get a degree
Change careers
Improve your finances
Learn how to invest your money
Start a business
Write a book
Start painting
Learn to meditate
Start doing yoga
Start an exercise program
Start eating more healthfully
Bring a life partner into your life
Create a safe, loving home environment
Establish a stronger connection with your divine self
Learn to work with your dreams
Develop your psychic abilities
Expand your ability to receive from the universe
Become more confident
Learn to speak your truth, be more assertive
Create more joy, love, peace, faith, hope, goodness and other God qualities, in your life

List Two—All the Things I Need to Get Done

This is easy. On a sheet of paper write down all the things you need to get done in your daily life. Again, use the mind map format if that works for you. In this list makes sure to include those projects you've been putting off for a long time.

Here's an example of what you might have on this list:

Organize the bedroom closet

Paint the living room

Clear your office desk drawers

Reorganize your kitchen

Research better insurance rates

Find a financial institution that pays higher interest rates

Mow the lawn

Clear the garage

Wash the car

Clean up the filing cabinet

When you make your lists, you will think of the most obvious things first. However, as time passes, more ideas will come to mind, especially those deeper desires. Make sure you write those down.

If it feels right, take a few days or a week to complete the lists. If you choose to give yourself this time, stay focused. Don't forget to get back to the lists; you want to make sure you give yourself the opportunity to create a more fulfilling life.

As you work on your lists, ideas may come to you at any time—at an odd moment during the day, at night before you fall asleep, in your dreams or when you wake up in the morning. This is very good. It means your inner self, your soul self is joining you in your intention to live your soul truth and is helping you. Stop and take a moment and be grateful for the help.

Above all, realize this important fact: You are experiencing a connection with your divine self! If one of your desires is to create a clear connection with your inner self, it becomes really important to notice when the connection takes place. This awareness immediately strengthens your connection. And that's what you want, an ever-expanding connection and communication with your divine aspect.

Most importantly, you can use this spontaneous moment of connection as a reference point. You can begin to understand what the connection to your divine self feels like and under what circumstance it took place and became apparent. You can then use this information to make the connection with your divine self even stronger. How wonderful is that? I love it!

Receiving spontaneous information from your divine self is one of the first steps toward you and your inner self working in partnership to create something in the world.

It is a very important step to notice, acknowledge and cultivate. Of course, write all those additional ideas down, regardless of how unusual or strange they may seem.

Very good. Now that you've made your lists how do you feel? Excited, I hope, even if possibly feeling some trepidation. That's all right. That's normal. As you progress, you'll get excited.

In starting your lists in this way, by directing your mind, directing, focusing your thought, you have begun to consciously harness the natural universal energy of creation, the natural tool of manifestation. You are on your way to fulfillment! How exciting!

Now let me show you the Planning System and how it works. Afterward we will begin to use it.

6.

The Planning System & How It Works

You are now ready to take further action on your intention to organize your life, fulfill your dreams and get things done. You will move your body in support of that intention by setting up the Planning System.

The Planning System is a simple but effective tool for planning and manifesting. Briefly, this is how you will set it up.

You will need a corkboard. You will cut small pieces of paper. On the pieces of paper you will write your projects and tasks and pin them on the corkboard. That's it. See the completed board at the end of the chapter.

Now, let's take it a step at a time.

You will need:
- 1 corkboard—about 36" x 24" or any size board that

works for you
- Paper, white and/or colored paper
- Pen or pencil
- Old magazines you can use to cut out pictures of your projects
- Drawing paper, if you choose to draw your projects
- Colored pencils and other art supplies you might need to draw your projects
- Tacks for the corkboard
- Scissors and/or paper cutter

Let's Set Up the Corkboard

Take your paper and cut nine pieces, about 1" x 1.25" each. You can decide what size works best for you.

On seven pieces of paper write out the days of the week, Sunday, Monday, Tuesday and so on. Or you can use your computer to type and print out the days and then cut them out.

On the remaining two pieces of paper write, "Current Projects" and "Gestation Projects." More about gestation projects in a minute.

Starting on the left side of the board, on top, tack the piece of paper called Gestation Projects. Then move to the right of the board and tack Current Projects. Continuing to the right, place the days of the week. When you're done, all your headings should spread out nicely across the top of the board.

Cut extra pieces of paper, about 1" x 1.25", maybe of a different color. You will use these to write out your projects and tasks and tack them on the corkboard. You can also use pictures or drawings. If so, you would put those up on the board. More about the value of using pictures and drawings next.

That's it, you're done setting up the corkboard.

Using Pictures, Drawings & Symbols to Represent Your Projects

When you start working with the corkboard, you will use the small pieces of paper to write down your projects and tack them on the board. However, if you like, and when it's possible, you can use pictures from magazines to represent your projects. You can also choose to draw or paint your projects. Or you might even want to use symbols to represent your projects—something that clearly evokes what you want to create, for example a big red heart for love.

It's up to you to decide how you represent your manifesting projects. However, there are some pretty powerful benefits to using pictures and drawings. This is how it works.

Keeping in mind that thought creates reality, as you page through magazines looking for the best picture for your project, you focus your thought for an extended period of time, you strengthen it, gather energy, making it faster to manifest in the physical realm. The same is true if you decide to draw a picture of your project.

You start to focus your thoughts as soon as you start to gather supplies to draw your project. Then you contemplate how best to represent your project through a drawing. As you draw it or paint it, your body and mind work together to create the drawing. With all these actions, you sustain focus, build thought, build energy, pulling your project into the physical realm.

However, there are even more benefits to having pictures and drawings of your project on your corkboard.

When you look at pictures on your corkboard, you bypass the left brain, the analytical brain. The picture sinks right into your consciousness. Think about what happens when you look at an analog clock as compared to a digital clock. With an analog clock your mind instantly registers the time unlike with a digital clock where the left side of your brain has to work to know the time. A picture is a powerful tool of consciousness.

Don't forget that's how I got that awful car—by looking at a picture.

So, if you have time and it feels good to you, find pictures for your projects and make drawings. You will have fun and, at the same time, strengthen and expedite your manifestation projects.

Gestation Projects

What's a gestation project? A gestation project is any

project you want to manifest but are not quite ready to start planning.

When you're done your corkboard will display main projects, gestation projects and action steps.

How the Planning System Works

In the next chapter, you will prioritize your lists and decide which projects to work on first. Then you will write your first project on the small piece of paper and put it on the corkboard underneath the heading, "Current Projects." If you decide to use a picture or a drawing for your project, you will first find a picture or make a drawing, then place it on the board.

You will determine your gestation projects and place those under the heading "Gestation Projects."

You will have specific tasks associated with your main projects. You will write the tasks on the small pieces of paper and place them on the corkboard. Tasks that have to be done on a specific day, go under that day. Tasks that can be done within the week go in the center of the week, toward the bottom of the board.

Let Spirit Guide You

Now, this is important. Creative and spiritual people tend to operate from intuition and inner guidance. We understand that spirit will guide us, if we ask, for best days and times to complete tasks. Our natural inclination is to move in harmony with that inner voice. Therefore, when you put a task up on the corkboard to be done within that week, you inform your inner self of your intention to accomplish this task and you create room for it to help you.

Your inner self will work on your task for you and guide you to the best times to accomplish the task. It will also guide you to optimal ways to accomplish it. In this way, you will not only move smoothly to complete your tasks but will also no longer operate only from your human personality. Instead, you will operate in partnership with your divine self.

Your divine self knows a whole lot more than you do. It can help you immeasurably. This is beyond fantastic. You will never feel alone. You will never be the only one having to figure it all out. There is always the presence of your divine self that can help you and offer the best possible advice that will be for your highest good.

Most importantly, when you work in partnership with your divine self, you become the divinity you seek. You are your divine self in a human body. You are who you are in truth: A divine human. You don't have to go somewhere to find yourself. You can begin to be your divine self starting with the simplest of life tasks. It's how you begin to integrate spirit and matter, live as a soul on earth.

Building Up Thought Energy

For anything to appear in matter, you have to have enough

thought energy—sort of a critical mass of thought energy that will bump your project from spirit into matter. How do you do this?

You focus your thought and build up energy by moving through the steps in working with the Planning System.

Looking at the board regularly, you focus your attention and build up thought energy. By moving your body to perform tasks related to your project, you focus your attention and build up thought energy.

When enough thought energy is built up, your project appears in the physical reality. You create. You manifest. You have success. You have fulfillment.

This is how you consciously work with the natural laws of the universe utilizing thought energy to create in the physical world and allowing room for your divine self to help.

To take full advantage of the Planning System, make sure you place your corkboard where you can easily see it, look at it and dream, i.e., focus and build thought. If necessary, carry it from room to room. I know this may be a little extreme, but if you've been frustrated about creating things in the world and getting things done, this is a small action to perform as a way to get in the flow of creating and accomplishing.

When you look at your corkboard, smile: You're a creator! You're being a co-creator with All That Is. You're creating what you love. You're making your life better. This is exciting.

When you start to use the Planning System, I recommend you use it in the manner I describe here. However, as you go along, pay attention to how it's working for you and adjust it in a way that works best for you. You can use a bigger board; use two boards; use different colors of paper, different shapes and sizes of paper and so on. Use it only for your main big projects—use it in whatever way works in the flow with your own makeup and in whatever way it is most helpful to you.

Lastly, let's not forget something important: Thought energy is God energy. In fact, another thing to keep in mind is that we, and everything else, is God energy. When we create, we use God energy. We did not invent the tool of thought, but we get to use it to build ourselves and our lives. If we keep this in mind, we can stay humble and grateful.

All right, we are ready to take a look at your lists, organize them and decide which projects to work on first. This will be fun! Onward we go.

Manifesting

Gestation Projects	Current Projects	Sunday	Monday	Tuesday	Wednesday	Thursday	Friday	Saturday

7.

Let's Manifest & Get Things Done!

We are now ready to implement the Planning System and make your desires a reality.

Let's prepare.

First, make sure you have plenty of time for this part of your manifesting process. You're releasing powerful forces; it's best that you are relaxed and don't feel hurried. Make sure you have privacy and that you won't be interrupted. You want to feel safe so you are free to dream. Have some beautiful music ready, if that feels supportive to you.

Next, gather what you need.

Get the two lists you made earlier. Get your tacks and small pieces of paper. Have extra paper near you and a pen or pencil. Get your magazines, if you plan to cut out pictures, and your drawing supplies if you plan to draw your projects. Have your corkboard in front of you.

I have a picture of a completed corkboard at the end of the chapter if you'd like to see what a completed board looks like.

Now get ready for some fun and satisfaction!

Choose Your First Project

We'll start with List One, your dreams and desires list. You are going to decide what you want to create first.

Slowly read through all the dreams you have on your list. Pay close attention to how you feel as you read each item. Your feelings are going to tell you what is most important to you. Notice what goes through your mind as you look at each item. Pay close attention to what happens in your body.

Now that you're about to make your dreams come true, many feelings may come up.

You may become aware of how you've neglected yourself and your dreams, how you regularly discounted the promptings of your soul. It may become obvious the way you've subordinated your wishes in favor of everyone else's.

All these insights and feelings may be painful to witness; however, they are invaluable. They are a powerful catalyst for change.

As hard as it may be to see and feel all this, just stay

with it. Give yourself time to feel all your feelings. Let them be without trying to change them, without any blame. Most importantly, don't suppress them. It may not be easy, but just remind yourself you are in the process of making your life better. How you feel this moment is temporary. Soon, everything will begin to get better.

Once you've moved through any difficult emotions, hopefully you will start to get excited about creating your desires.

Looking at your list, what did you discover? Which projects feel urgent, important? Which projects make you light up, make your heart sing, fill you with excitement?

With projects that ring true at the deepest level, you might experience a sense of exhilaration, expansion, a feeling of being one with the whole universe, a sense of having no boundaries, no limits.

On a separate piece of paper, write down all the projects that make you feel this way.

Now, let's narrow down the list.

Choose one to three projects that feel most exciting and most fun, that create most illumination in your being.

Very good.

Now choose one project you would like to manifest first.

The idea of making this project a reality should fill

you with joy, love, energy, enthusiasm. You should feel terrific about making this project a reality.

If your project is about changing a life condition, you should feel overwhelming relief and vibrant hope that you're about to improve your life.

Make Sure You *Really* Want to Create This Project

At this point, take time and make sure you *really* want to create this project, because if you are diligent in using the Planning System *you will create it*. Make every effort to be clear that this creation is for your absolute highest good on all levels, physical, emotional, mental and spiritual. If you need to, spend time, a day or two, seeking guidance from your divine self as to the wisdom of creating this project.

Ideally, you want to manifest projects that expand your life, bring you to a higher level of being, higher consciousness. If your material projects satisfy this requirement, they will serve you in the best way possible. If they do not, they can become burdensome appendages that can get in the way of your greatest good.

When you are ready, write the name of your chosen project on the small piece of paper. Tack it on the corkboard under "Current Projects." If you decide to use a picture or make a drawing, do that first, then tack it on the board.

If you have a dream you want to fulfill and you are really excited about it, but see absolutely no way how you could possibly fulfill that dream, I encourage you to go ahead and place it on your board regardless. As you take steps toward creating your dream, your divine self will help and come up with ideas, people and opportunities you could never ever have imagined, and you will make your dream a reality.

Let's Make a Mind Map & Identify Steps You Need to Take to Make Your Project a Reality

Next, we will break down your project into steps you need to take to have what you want or achieve the change you seek.

We will start by making a mind map.

Take a sheet of paper. In the middle of the paper write the name of your project. Now list all the things you can think of that you need to do to make your project a reality.

Example Project: Machu Picchu Vacation

As an example, let's say your project is a dream vacation to Machu Picchu.

The first thing you would do is to place "Trip to Machu Picchu" on your corkboard under the "Current Project" heading. If you're using a picture or your own drawing, you would put that on the board.

Next, you will make a mind map and list all the things you will need to do to get to Peru.

Here is a list of things you might have to do to find

yourself with a camera and good hiking gear on Machu Picchu:
- Go to the library and bookstore and get books on Machu Picchu.
- Visit a travel agent to learn about traveling to Peru.
- Research travel companies on the Internet offering trips to Machu Picchu.
- Research best time of the year to travel to Machu Picchu.
- Find out how and where to get a passport, if you don't already have one.
- See if you need a visa or any other documents to travel to Peru.
- Research if you need to have any shots.
- Get a calculator and add up what it will cost to take the trip. Include airplane tickets; shots (if any); passport cost; clothes, shoes, backpack, luggage; spending money once you're there; accommodations; the cost of a tour company, if you are using one, and any other expenses you can think of.
- Check to see when you can take off work.
- Think about who will take care of your dog or your house or anything else that might need attending while you're away.

Identify the Very First Step You Need to Take to Make Your Dream a Reality

All right, say you've made a mind map and listed all the things you need to do to make your project a reality. Now look at your mind map and see what you need to do first or several things you can do right away.

For my Peru example, I would say the place to start is to research Machu Picchu. Now, that's a good first step in planning, but you want something even better. You want to identify the very first concrete step you can take to begin to make your project a reality. In this case, the very first step might be to go to the bookstore and the library and get some books about Machu Picchu. That action step would go on the corkboard.

It's important that your corkboard have clear and specific action steps. That way, when you look at the board, you will know exactly what action you need to take. You don't have to think about it and figure it out.

If, for example, you had pinned on your board, do Machu Picchu research, you'd be left wondering what specifically you needed to do. It's unlikely you'd stop and take the time to figure it out, so you will do nothing to make your project a reality. This lack of specificity as to the exact action will stall you out every time. You want to be able to glance at your board and know immediately what you need to do. No thinking required. So, on your board pin only clear action steps. That's what will get you to where you want to go.

Have you decided on your first action step? What is it?

Place Your Action Steps on the Board

Where on the corkboard do you pin your action step of going to the library in my Machu Picchu example?

If you know for sure you will go to the library on a certain day, tack the piece of paper right under that day. If you are uncertain, because you have other things going on and you will do it when it's in the flow, pin the paper toward the bottom of the board and in the middle of the week.

Once your task is up on the board, you will see it daily and, as the week progresses, there will be the perfect time to stop at the library. It will be in the perfect flow with your other errands.

You may have other tasks you want to accomplish during that week. You would write those out on the little pieces of paper and put them on the board, either under a particular day, to get done that day, or in the center near the bottom, to get done sometime during the week.

Placing tasks on your corkboard to get done sometime within the week, on the energy level, accomplishes several things. Once up on the board, you will not forget to do them. Every day you will look at your board and see your tasks. Your mind will register them, your thoughts will build up, your inner self will help you with your intention and, at some point during the week, your intuition will guide you to the perfect day and the perfect time and you will accomplish your task.

Once you start taking action on your project, momentum will build. You will get more ideas and automatically go to the next and the next step eventually having what you desired. You will have success in actualizing your dream!

Excellent. Now let's say you want to create something abstract, like develop your psychic abilities. How would you do that?

Planning Abstract Projects

Planning abstract projects involves some additional steps. Here are some examples of how you might handle them.

Example Project: Develop Psychic Abilities

You start the same way as a concrete project. You write "Develop my psychic abilities" and pin that on the board under Current Projects.

Then you get a big sheet of paper and in the center write: "Develop my psychic abilities." Now see what comes to mind as to how you can do that.

Your list might look something like this:
- Go to the library and bookstore and look for books on developing psychic abilities.
- Research schools on the Internet that offer psychic development classes.
- Find psychics and talk to them about developing your own psychic abilities.

These are great beginning steps. However, since this project is about your own personal development and since this personal development involves your divine self in an important way, a few additional steps might be helpful. These steps are similar to the steps I outlined in the chapter on establishing communication with your divine self.

Here are additional steps you might wish to take as a way to develop your psychic abilities:
- Journal about your desire to develop psychic abilities and what this means to you.
- Before you go to bed at night, ask your divine self to help you open this ability.
- Listen to guided meditations that are about making a stronger connection with your divine self.

You would add these steps to your mind map, then choose your first action step, maybe go to the library to do some research. That would go on your board. You might also want to journal about what developing psychic abilities means to you.

All right, very good. Now let's take another example, something even more abstract.

Example Project: Create Peace in Your Life

Let's say what matters most to you right now is to have peace in your life. Upon reflection, you might have realized your life has been a bumpy ride with lots of turmoil and upset and you're sick of it. You realize that, more than anything, you want peace in your life so you can relax, enjoy being alive.

You pin that project on your corkboard and you pull out your big sheet of paper and in the middle write: "Peace in my life." All around the central heading you would list everything you can think of that you can do to create peace in your life.

This is a big inner transformation you are seeking, effecting every area of your life. Part of creating peace in your life might involve resolving and healing childhood issues that have been the cause of continuous chaos and turmoil. Therefore, your mind map might look somewhat different from the other two.

It might look something like this:
- Examine and journal about actions you take and things you say that take away peace.
- Journal about what peace means to you; see if you come to an inner feeling place where you can formally commit to having a peaceful life.
- Listen to guided meditations that are about establishing peace.
- Read some books on living a successful, joyful life.
- Before you go to bed at night, let your inner self know you would like to have peace in your life and ask for help in creating it.

- Talk to a therapist about having a peaceful life.

Look at your mind map and see which action step you'd like to take first, or a couple of them, maybe journaling about what peace means to you and listening to a guided meditation about peace. Pin those on the board.

What Are Your Abstract Projects?

Take a look at your list. Do you have any abstract projects you would like to actualize? Put them up on the board under Current Projects, make a mind map, identify first steps and put them on the board. Very good.

Gestation Projects

You will most likely have a few gestation projects. Here is an example of how to work with gestation projects.

Example Gestation Project: Love in My Life

Maybe it is love you want in your life, but you are not yet ready to address this. You proceed as with current projects and write "Love in my life" and tack it on the corkboard under "Gestation Projects." You don't need to make a mind map for your gestation projects.

Once your project is on the board, you will see it daily. Energy will build up. And, most likely, you will begin to experience positive changes right away—even though you will have taken no specific action to manifest this project, except for this: You identified what you wanted/needed, set an intention to create it and tacked it on the board.

Yes, even without you taking specific action, except for having an intention and pinning it on the board, seeing that desire on the board will automatically gather your energy and start to bring about the results you desire. Being aware of what you want and believing you can create it is a powerful state of consciousness.

Example Gestation Project: Buy House

One of your gestation projects may be something material, like buying a house. You will tack that on the corkboard. Every day you will see "Buy house" on your board or see the picture or drawing. Every day you will build up your thought energy. At some point, you will have an experience.

You may decide you don't want a house after all. Or a house may come up on sale that you can afford and that's perfect for you and you go and buy it.

Or other things may happen that will, in some way, clarify your project.

It may be that you need to move to a different state for a job and buying a house where you currently live is no longer in the plan.

It may be that some time passes and you feel ready to actively start the process of house hunting. At that point, you will begin to identify all the things you need to do to buy a house. You will decide on first steps and pin them on the corkboard and continue to take steps until you have your house.

Identify Your Gestation Projects

Look at your list and see if there are things you want, but just can't get to them right away. Write them down on the small piece of paper and tack them under Gestation Projects. A couple of gestation projects are good. More than that, given the fact that you'll be working on your main projects, might be overload. If you have time, you can use pictures and drawings.

Naming Your Projects

Remember, you are creating something, building something, so when you give a name to your project, make sure it's a name that's about creating.

Say you want to lose weight. The name of your project would not be "lose weight." That would be difficult to create. However, what you can create is a slim, agile, strong body. So your project name might be "Create a slim body."

For all your projects make sure you get clear on what you want to create, something you can build, make happen—not something you don't want or something or somebody you want to get away from. Your mind and your divine self can work with a clear picture of something you want to create. And don't forget to use pictures and drawings for your projects, if that feels right for you.

At this point, if you've worked on your own manifestation projects along with my examples, you will have on your corkboard: Current and gestation projects and tasks associated with those projects.

I am sure you see the entire pattern how, by using the Planning System, you can organize yourself, stay focused on your projects and tasks, build thought energy and allow room for your divine self to help—until your projects emerge into physical reality.

I want to take a moment here to encourage you to identify qualities and conditions you would like to have into your life and make them your manifestation projects. If you're not quite ready for some of them, pin them in the gestation area of the board.

Qualities and conditions of being underpin every other manifestation. If you have those established in a way that matches God energies, creating all else will be easier.

I would also like to encourage you to look at your life conditions. If there is an area of your life where you have been unhappy for a long time, start to think about improving it. Yes, this unhappy situation may have lasted so long you've lost hope of it ever changing; nevertheless, make the effort. Don't deprive yourself of happiness by not taking action. You *do* have the power to change undesirable conditions—if you set your intention to do so. By making them projects you work on consciously, identifying first steps, taking action and staying the course, you are sure to have success.

List Two—Let's Prioritize Tasks

All right, we are ready to move on to the second list. This should be easy.

Look at your list. What is urgent and has to get done immediately?

Let's say you've been delaying tuning up your car and it's really important that you get this done as soon as possible.

Now, identify the very first step you need to take to tune up your car. That would be: "Call shop and make appointment." Write that down on your piece of paper and put it on the corkboard.

Go down your task list and note everything that is a priority. Identify the very first step. Write it down and put it up on the board.

Do this with as many tasks as you can do in one week. Then start, again, the following week.

As you get tasks done, remove them from the corkboard and put up new tasks.

With tasks right there in front of you, your mind will register them and at some point, it will be the perfect time to do them.

Now, as you go down your task list, you might realize some of your tasks are actually big projects requiring numerous steps. If that's the case, pin the project on the corkboard under Current Projects, make a mind map, identify first steps and pin those on the corkboard.

Very good. What you now have on your corkboard are clearly identified long-term projects, short-term projects and immediate tasks. Some projects are active, some in gestation. At a glance, you can see all of them on your board.

When you achieve success with a project and feel ready, move on to the next project and go through the same process. Create a mind map, identify first steps and take action.

You keep moving forward, actualizing your dreams, manifesting concrete things, converting challenges into wants, bringing great qualities into your life, continuously improving life conditions and staying on top of daily must-do tasks.

This is how you work with the natural laws of the universe to create in the world: Following your soul promptings, focusing the energy of your thought, allowing your divine self to help—to create in the world. It is wonderful to consciously create in this way. It is wonderful to witness the power of your soul in the world. The satisfaction of creation is tremendous. However, what is most incredible about this way of creating is how you will feel. You will feel the power of your soul as it is connected to All That Is. This brings a sense of unprecedented harmony and oneness within yourself as human and divine, at the same time—in the world.

Some Suggestions

- Make sure you really want to create your project.
- Make sure you don't have too many projects going on at once.
- Have your corkboard where you can always see it.
- Look at your board regularly.
- Continually update your board.

Keep Track of Your Manifesting Successes

Most of us are busy with life. You will certainly be busy once you start using the Planning System. You'll be moving from creation to creation, manifesting concrete things, bringing in great new qualities and improving life conditions. This is excellent. And what is really good and important to do is to stop once in a while and take inventory of all that you have created. If you do this, you will be astounded to discover just how much you have accomplished and how much you have grown.

I recommend you set up a "My Successful Manifestations" notebook or page. Every time you complete a project, write it down on this list and celebrate. I have also provided couple of blank pages at the end of the book for you to record your successes, if you wish.

If you write down each successful manifestation, you will be encouraged to continue to create and you will remind yourself of just how powerful a creator you are. You will remind yourself that yes, you can create most anything, heal most anything, change most any life condition for the better, bring in yet another wonderful God quality into your life. And this is wonderful, indeed!

Time

It is really important to allow enough time for manifestation to happen. I will talk more about that later but wanted to mention it here because this is such an important part of the manifesting process.

Generally, when we don't get something we want pretty quickly, we begin to think that we will never get it. We are inclined to move into the mindset, a state of consciousness of "I'll never have it"—undermining ourselves and our original intention to create that thing. Try to remember that focus of thought has to be sustained, sometimes for a long period of time, for you to create what you want.

Naturally, when we're in a painful or difficult situation, we all want instant relief, we all want instant change. That may not always be possible. As hard as it may be, try to be patient. Sustain the focus. Have faith in the great divine. Expect the most positive outcome. When doubts and concerns arise, face them directly and neutralize them; clear your aura of anything that might be in the way of your creation. Be willing to learn whatever lessons you need to learn in the situation. Be willing to change. And, hopefully soon, you will have manifestation.

Also, some manifestations, usually about qualities or abilities or the expression of life purpose, tend to take a long time. When the manifestation happens, you may not even remember when you initiated the process of creation. Nevertheless, try to notice when you finally have something you wanted a long time ago. This will help you keep things in perspective, help you understand that creation happens over an entire lifetime, in fact, over lifetimes. This will give you confidence, make you stronger and validate just how powerful a creator you are.

What if You Try & Try & Can't Create What You Want?

There are many reasons why you might not be able to create what you want. Here are a few:

- What you want is not in alignment with your soul purpose. In other words, you may want something so off your soul path, there simply isn't enough energy to create it. This may be a situation where you think you want something or believe it is the right thing to want and create, when, deep down, you feel something very different. If this happens, the solution is to find a way to know your deepest truth.
- You may not be able to create something you want because you have too many countering thoughts and beliefs that say you can't, beliefs that may have originated in

childhood and of which you are not conscious. If this happens, you'll need to heal the childhood core beliefs so your project can manifest. There are different ways to do this. Seeing a therapist is one of them. If you like guided meditations, I've designed Healing Core Energies to specifically handle this situation.

- Another reason you may not be able to create what you want is because the time is not right. If that's the case, usually other things need to happen first. Usually, those other things are about growing you in important ways that allow manifestation to take place at a later date.
- You may not be able to manifest a project because you may not be taking any action and therefore not building up enough thought energy for creation.
- Your project may simply take longer than you thought.
- You may not be able to create what you want because of spiritual reasons that are often difficult to identify, such as karma or plans the soul made before incarnation.

All right. Now, let's talk about something very important—the biggest obstacle you might face on your journey to manifesting your desires and creating a grander life, a grander you: Your unwillingness, albeit unconscious, to receive a grander life. Let's make sure this does not stop you.

	Sunday	Monday	Tuesday	Wednesday	Thursday	Friday	Saturday
Gestation Projects							
Current Projects							
Buy House	Machu Picchu Vacation						
More Love in my Life		Library Research Machu Picchu		Call Make Appt. Oil Change			
					Org. Filing Cabinet	Wash Car	

8.

Be Willing to Change, Be Willing to Receive a Grander Life

What is the biggest obstacle to having a grander life? Not being willing to receive a grander life.

Surprising, isn't it?

Why is this the case?

There are many reasons. The main reason is fear of change.

Years ago, when I was doing research for my dissertation, I came across an unbelievable statistic: People would rather die than change.

On and off since then I have reflected on this unbelievable statistic until the obvious hit me. There are numerous people unwilling to quit smoking even though they have been told they are in danger if they don't. Same with weight loss. People endanger their lives by being overweight and are still unwilling to take action to make a change. These are simple, prevalent examples of the way people would rather die than change.

In other situations, people are not willing to make the effort to change simply because they do not know how good they can feel emotionally and physically if they made the change, how much better their lives would be. They have never experienced a great level of well-being, so there is little motivation to make the necessary effort.

Now let's look more closely at the process of change.

Fear of Change

In psychic reading sessions, I look at the human aura, the human energy field. That field is very much set up. In a certain way, you could say, it's solidly in place. This is the person's identity. This is the person's reality in the world. The person is used to being who they are. It is the only reference point she has in the world, a way to function in the world. To make any change would mean a loss of the known reality. And since the human personality has to maintain a grip on physical reality in order to function, it is easy to see how change would be frightening.

Furthermore, when we change, we become someone new. The old self dissolves, dies. This is a painful process to go through. We mourn the loss of a self we have known, even though a new, potentially more conscious, self is born.

Of course, we are also afraid of change because we don't know what we will find when we get to our destination. The unknown scares us.

Given these many obstacles to change, the tendency is not to make any change at all, not to start on a new journey at all. We often opt for the safe known, even if it is misery, rather than embark into the unknown.

Change is a Means of Growth

Nevertheless, change is the one constant, not only in our earthly life but also in the larger Reality. It is a means of growth and expansion in the universe. Your soul grows, expands and evolves. All That Is grows and expands and evolves—while always being all that It could be; yes, a paradox, but we won't venture to understand that right now.

Given the fact that none of us can escape change, how do we deal with change in a way that is constructive?

First, you keep in mind that all of us are afraid of change to a different degree. And you keep in mind why we are afraid—loss of reality, loss of self, fear of the unknown and so on.

Simply understanding why we are afraid of change makes all the difference. Unconscious fear won't control us; fear won't stop us from moving forward.

Next, you learn how to do change in a way that you can handle. And that actually is not so difficult:

You do change slowly.

How to Make Change Slowly

You make change by taking one small step at a time.

First, you formally decide you want to make the change.

Next, you give yourself time to adjust to the idea that you're about to make a change.

Then you start to take steps.

In psychic reading sessions I have seen that the human personality, next to the person's soul, is like a little child, a very small child, really. For the human personality to feel safe and secure, you have to attend to and address all of its fears. You cannot ignore the emotions, the anxieties and concerns of the human personality. If you do, they will make it difficult for you to move forward.

Journal as a Way to Neutralize Fears and Anxieties

A good way to handle the concerns of the human personality is to talk to someone about them and to journal.

In journaling write about the change you are planning; about any fears, doubts, concerns—what you think might or might not happen; why you are anxious—what you worry might or might not happen, and so on.

As you journal, pay attention to signals from your body. They will let you know how you feel about this proposed change. Notice if you tense up, if you're holding your breath, if you start to fidget or want to get up and get something to eat or go to the bathroom or make a call, and so on. Then directly face this discomfort and discover what it's about.

When you stop and address the concerns of your personality in this way, you will find that much of the trepidation leaves immediately. This scared and anxious part of you just needs to be recognized and heard. You'll find that, most of the time, what you've feared is generally nothing much to be afraid of and that you can handle it. Underneath that fear you might be surprised to discover excitement and enthusiasm about your upcoming journey.

Once you've given time for your human personality to get used to the fact that you're embarking on a journey, physical or internal, you can begin to take practical steps toward your goal.

As you take steps, continue to stay alert to fears and anxieties. The more aware you are of your feelings and concerns and take time to address them, the easier it will be to move forward.

What will also help you make the change you desire is to imagine this new life you are creating.

Imagine the New Life You Are Creating as a Way to Bring New Energies into Your Aura

Your present life is a set of energies. The you in this present life is used to having only so much, thinking a certain way, having certain expectations from life and people. You operate at a certain level of contentment or discontentment, a certain level of happiness or unhappiness. You are used to this vibration, this frequency. You are used to feeling this way. You may not know any other way to feel.

When you begin your journey toward more joy, peace, love, success, contentment and the like, you move into a higher vibration. You expand. You hold more energy. You become a new you. Ultimately your life will be bigger. You will have more power. You will wield a bigger brush stroke in life, have greater influence. In this larger life, you will have even greater opportunity to grow with these new resources, energy and power. Your potential for expansion expands.

Since you've never been there before, how do you know what it will feel like? You imagine it.

There are many ways to do this. You can use guided meditations to envision this new life. You can create a vision board where you paste pictures and drawings of your new life. You can journal. In your visioning, you would include all aspects of this new life: How it looks, how it feels, how you would behave in the world and with people. You will want to make these images expansive, filled with God qualities: Joy, love, peace, harmony, contentment, satisfaction, vitality, exuberance, prosperity, lightness of being and so on.

By focusing on these positive energies, you bring them into your aura. You begin to get used to feeling this greater sense of well-being, this higher vibration. I can't overemphasize how important this is. By imagining and feeling these qualities, you train yourself to live in this higher vibration that will allow you have this grander life.

This process of envisioning is analogous to the training an athlete undertakes to excel in her chosen sport. She trains to create a strong, agile body capable of exceptional performance.

You also train to achieve more, be a grander you with a grander life, by using your imagination to expand your aura, your being, move into a higher frequency of being.

Training yourself in this way, you also take away the fear from the human personality; it now knows where you're going. It's familiar with the new energies and the new reality.

By taking time to imagine these new energies, it becomes easier to take the steps you need to take to make the change you desire that will lead to having what you want. So, take time to dream as a way to create what you want.

It goes without saying that with this effort and focus, your inner self has time to come in and help. Any time you have a clear intention and take steps, your divine self is available with ideas and support. You just need to listen and accept the guidance.

Change is a Process of Transformation; Give Yourself the Needed Time

Most of my clients expect quick change. I think we are all so used to instant everything, we forget that certain things in life take time and cannot be hurried.

Change, at the deepest level, is an organic process of transformation. One small change in attitude sets a new platform that allows other change to happen. Once that change happens, other change becomes possible.

You cannot skip steps and you cannot hurry the transformation.

Give yourself about a year to make a big change. If the issue is really deep and complicated, give yourself more time. The fact is, if you make the decision to make the change and if you sustain the focus, you will most likely succeed unless there are some deeper, unidentified energies at work.

Again, we are used to things happening fast and it is hard for us to stay focused on something for a year or more. However, the effort is always worth it. You will have overcome some lifelong problem and will be free to live a new life of lightness of being. Or you will have created something you desired for a long time and will feel unprecedented satisfaction. Best of all, these efforts will open your energy field and make it possible for you to have more wonderful experiences.

Remember, though, you have to want that lightness of

being, that new you, that expanded self. You have to be willing to change. You have to be willing to go through the discomfort the process of change requires.

I know most of us will always say Yes! When asked if we want some positive change. But is that really true at the deepest level? Your human personality can easily say yes, but what is happening with that deeper part of your being that is afraid of change? That part of you will almost always decide whether a change happens or not. This is why you have to prepare for change.

Here's an example I like to give my clients about the process of moving from their current lives to grander lives and what it's like when we try to hurry or force a change for which we are not prepared.

Imagine you are living in a nice, cozy cottage. It stands on a large property where there is also a castle. From your cottage, in the distance, you can see the castle. Daily you look at the castle and shake your head and say, "Boy, that is grand, I wish I lived there," and you sigh. When friends come and visit and say, "Don't you wish you lived in the castle?" you always say, "Of course, anybody would want to live there." Then one day, there is a knock on your door and you see three men standing there. "Ready?" one of them says. "We're moving you into the castle. You'll have all the freedom to run it just as you like. Let's go."

I am positive you'll say, "Ah, well, hold on, I don't

know if I want to move into the castle." You look around your cozy little cottage, the comfort of it, think lovingly of how over the years you've made it a home. Through your mind run things like, "What am I going to do in that humongous stone thing? How will I keep it warm? How will I pay the bills? How will I clean it?"

You tell the three men, "No, thank you. I'm staying here." Then they get a little nasty, "You're moving whether you like it or not," and they start to haul your furniture.

You scream, you try to stop them, you're beyond yourself with fear.

Well, that's what it's like for the human personality when you try to hurry or force a change. It will panic and resist.

However, if you prepare for the journey, you will be ready. In this example of moving to the castle, if you had the time to resolve your concerns about living in the castle, you might have become excited to expand your life in such a grand way.

The moral of the story: Don't deprive yourself of a greater life by trying to make change happen faster than your human personality can handle.

Is there a change you've tried to make, again and again, and repeatedly failed? Think back: Have you leaped with a giant burst of energy, trying to make it happen all at once, instead of taking your time and taking small steps?

Try again. This time take the smallest steps possible. Give yourself lots of time to make the change. This is especially important when there are childhood issues involved. Look at it as a long-term project. Stay focused and keep going until you achieve your goal.

Make Changes Promptly When Needed

The other side of this story is delaying making a change when one is urgently needed.

As I've already said, the universe uses change to help us grow and evolve. Since there is nothing you can do about this universal principle, it is good to accept change and not fight it.

The best way to do this is to stay alert to when a change is needed and take prompt action.

As I am sure you know, and have possibly experienced, when we are unwilling to make a necessary change, whether external or internal, in the end, the universe will do it for us. It will force dramatic change on us.

You know the story . . . you ignore the change you need to make and the universe does a little nudge by bringing about an unpleasant situation as a way to get you going. You ignore the nudge. Some time passes and maybe you get a bigger nudge, something even more unpleasant. If you ignore that, you get the proverbial two by four where you are knocked off your feet and totally out of commission or are forced into the exact situation or environment you've been trying to avoid.

Don't wait for the universe to force a change on you. Stay alert to the changes you need to make and consistently and promptly make them.

Here are some examples of situations where a change was needed and not made and the resultant consequences:

- You hate your job but are not doing anything to make it better. The job gets more unpleasant; you still do nothing. Then one day you get fired. To spare yourself all this stress and anguish, the minute you notice you're unhappy with your job, start to do something about it.
- You live on the financial edge. No money in savings. You keep thinking you need to do something about this but don't take any action. One day you lose your job, can't pay the rent and are in a serious crisis. If you're worried about your finances, take action immediately.
- You live with your boyfriend. You're not happy with the relationship. You don't have a job. You know you should do something about all of it but you do nothing. One day your boyfriend tells you he found someone new and wants you to move out. You have no job. You have no money. You have no place to go. Again, as soon there is unhappiness, worry, anxiety, take action right away.

I've learned many things by giving psychic readings

and one of the most important things I've learned is that we can spare ourselves most of our grief in life if we take action the minute something is not working in our lives. This way we don't let the situation become a crisis. In crisis, we are forced to deal with all the issues we refused to deal with earlier—all at once!

On the other hand, if we address the situation the minute it becomes a problem, we can work through it constructively and productively and grow and evolve from the experience, as we are meant to do.

Now that you'll be using the Planning System, perhaps your first order of business, your first manifestation project, might be to identify and resolve the most troubling, worrisome, anxiety-producing situations in your life. That is what I would strongly recommend. If you do this, you will spare yourself bigger problems down the road.

Summary

- Be willing to have a grander life.
- Be willing to change.
- Fear is normal when it comes to change. You learn to live with it and don't let it stop you from moving forward.
- Journal or talk to someone about your fears and concerns as a way to get past them.
- Do change slowly. Take small steps.
- If something isn't working in your life, take immediate

action and make appropriate changes.
- If you've tried and tried to make a change and failed, try again. This time manage your fears and anxieties. Take tiny steps.
- Use the Planning System to address your most-urgent worries and concerns and create a better life for yourself.

9.

Parting Words

We are at the end of our journey together, for me a pleasant and privileged journey, and here I would like to share with you some last thoughts and perspectives.

In writing this book I became keenly aware of the fact that self-help and spiritual books, by virtue of the medium, can make things sound simple and even easy, when in fact they are not, neither simple nor easy. And this is definitely true for the Planning System. Moving into more light, more power, more fulfillment, as good as it sounds, can be a challenge. And it is as much a challenge for me as it is for anybody else.

Psychically I see how energy operates and how manifestation and transformation happen, so I know, without any doubt and with great clarity, how the whole process works. However, it is still a challenge to live the principles in daily life.

First, habits exist and get in the way. Second, witnessing the effectiveness of the Planning System is positively unnerving. The successful manifestations demonstrate, in no uncertain terms, the kind of power that is within us, the truth of our divinity. That's a lot to get used to.

Nevertheless, this does not change the fact that with this knowledge we are in a privileged position. We know that we create our reality. We know how energy operates in the human energy field to create our reality. We know how to create. This is pure power. Ultimate freedom. And a huge responsibility.

Not knowing how we create our reality can be torment and suffering. We move around in darkness unable to understand why certain things happen, why we can't fix a problem or why we can't get what we want.

Yes, we are in a privileged position, living in grace. I recommend you use this knowledge for your highest good and the highest good of all.

I would also like to share with you something interesting that happened while I was writing this book. It was an urgency to tell you: Do not accept conditions and circumstances that are intolerable—even if they have been that way for a long, long time. You can make things better! Even in the most adverse and painful life conditions there is always a way to change something so things are in some way better. After that you continue to make the effort to make things even better.

In more "normal" life situations, you can actively begin to change unhappy circumstances for the better.

I find that it is of utmost importance, and of great help, to keep in mind these truths about yourself:

- You are a magnificent being of light, an aspect of All That Is.
- You are endowed with the same attributes of All That Is: You are a powerful creator. You create with your thought, with your mind.
- You are soul first and personality second. Your soul, your divine aspect can help you create what is of highest good for yourself and for everyone else.

The Planning System is here to organize you and help you create what you need and desire using the truth about who you are and the principles of the universe. Take some time, set it up and begin to create.

It may be difficult to fathom and accept the power that you have. That's okay. Just go slowly.

It may be difficult to believe that you may be able to change unhappy circumstances. That's okay. Proceed anyway and go slowly.

Go slowly with anything that scares you and where you have doubts. It takes time to get used to that much power.

And that much goodness.

As I said earlier, we have habits. We think in certain ways, believe certain things, assume certain things, go about our day in a certain way. To begin to change those habits and move in directions of conscious, constructive creation is no small task. So, go slowly. But keep going.

You don't have to do it perfectly. The only important thing is to keep going. Seemingly small efforts in physical reality, in energy reality, are giant leaps. Small efforts equal big intentions; our divine self understands intentions and will come in and help us.

If you have desired something for a long time, don't put off creating it. Use the Planning System to make it a reality. Don't deprive yourself of joy and fulfillment by not taking action to fulfill your dreams. Try to love yourself as your Creator loves you Who always wants only your highest good. That means being gentle with yourself and continuously aspiring to good for yourself and others.

Now I wish you the heady, palpable experience of your soul power, the supreme ecstasy of being a conscious creator with All That Is and the sublime peace that comes from being in attunement with all the universe.

A Meditation

Find a quiet place, put on some beautiful, heart-opening music and read the meditation. Allow yourself to be filled with the beauty and power of your divine self.

Or, if you like, you can listen to the audio version, set to music, of this guided meditation go to www.thetimeoflight.com, Downloads.

Use password: *__BookDownloads__*

I am a beautiful being of light.
Everywhere I look, there are opportunities. Everywhere I look, there are opportunities for the expansion of my potential and for fulfillment of all my being.
I feel soft in my heart for that is the place I receive all the goodness of the universe, all my good, where I hear the answers to all my needs, where the fulfillment of my soul unfolds.
I am soft now to receive all that feeds me, all that nurtures me.
I accept the love that is everywhere around me. I feel it spread through my body, healing it, enlivening it, illuminating my thoughts, illuminating my emotions.
I now feel the clear channel to my soul, feel the light

pouring through me. I am light.

I am at One with All That Is.

All knowledge is available to me, and I now open to receive, to accept the gift of consciousness, awareness, higher thoughts and perceptions.

I am One with All That Is.

I am boundless.

Love, joy, peace, creativity, and unfoldment, are the condition of my being. I revel in it, am swept clean of all lower vibrations, am made anew in the light of my true self.

Goodness is in me, everywhere around me and flows through all of creation. I now see that. I now feel that. I now accept that.

I am the creator of that goodness in my life and in everyone I touch.

Every day I open to more and more goodness in my life, more and more love.

Every day I see more and more opportunities to receive love and more and more opportunities to give love.

I soften, I open my heart when things get tough and answers flow through me—the path of goodness and light, integrity and truth.

I accept the goodness that is me and I let it radiate in the world so others can blossom.

I am love.
I am loved.
I love.
Peace.

The Planning System

- Make a list of your desires and dreams, abstract and concrete.
- From that list choose one project to create; tack the project on the corkboard under Current Projects.
- Create a mind map. Write everything you can think of that you need to do to accomplish this goal.
- From the mind map choose the very first action step. Pin it on the board either under a particular day to accomplish that day or towards the bottom of the board to accomplish when it's in the flow of other tasks.
- Identify an important project you are not ready to address immediately but would, nevertheless, like to get started on. Pin it on the board under Gestation Projects.
- Make a list of basic life tasks and chores.
- Choose the most important tasks you would like to accomplish and tack them on the board, either under a particular day or toward the bottom of the board.
- If a task is too big to accomplish in one action, it becomes a project. You pin it under Current Projects. Make a mind map, identify all steps you need to take to complete the project. Choose the first action step. Pin it on the board.
- Take action and get done all tasks you have on your board. When they are done, take them off the board.
- Look at your mind maps. Add new action steps to the board. Get those tasks done.

Quick Reference Guide

- Continue to work on your projects and get things done until you have success.
- Move on to the next project. Make mind maps. Put up action steps on your board. Get the tasks done.
- As you accomplish each manifestation, write it down on your list of successful creations.
- Always keep in mind: You're an aspect of All That Is, a divine human, a magnificent being of light, a powerful co-creator with the Creator.
- Enjoy being a creator!

Supporting Material

The Workings of Energy in the Human Energy Field: A Psychic's Perspective, Zorica Gojkovic, Ph.D.—This short book offers a detailed explanation of how energy operates in the human energy field and how this relates to the physical world and the divine.

Getting Things Done: The Art of Stress-Free Productivity, David Allen—A close look at the process of getting things done, including identifying that very crucial first step.

One Small Step Can Change Your Life, Robert Maurer, Ph.D.—When it's hard for us to do something we don't want to do or make changes we don't want to make, identifying the smallest action we can take, can bring about big change. This book deals with the psychological aspect of taking that first step.

Feel the Fear . . . and Do It Anyway: Dynamic Techniques for Turning Fear, Indecision, and Anger into Power, Action, and Love, Susan Jeffers, Ph.D.—I think the title explains it all.

Organizing From the Inside Out: The Foolproof System for Organizing Your Home, Your Office and Your Life, Julie Morgenstern—How to organize your space is a wonderful skill to have. It is something anyone can learn.

Time Management from the Inside Out: The Foolproof System for Taking Control of Your Schedule—and Your Life, Julie Morgenstern—Morgenstern helps you organize your time in a similar fashion she organizes space, by making the point that if you identify how much time a project requires, you'll get the project done.

Nonviolent Communication: A Language of Life, Marshall B. Rosenberg, Ph.D.—This is an important, powerful book. Not only do you learn an effective style of communication but in the process, you also heal your deepest childhood issues. Highly recommended.

Assertiveness: How to Be Strong in Every Situation, Conrad and Suzanne Potts—The Potts identify one critical point in being able to be assertive and that is knowing what you really want at the deepest level of your being. After that, it's easier to take action.

Evening Peace: A Guided Meditation, Zorica Gojkovic, Ph.D.— Identify and clear concerns of the day and focus on where you are going. Powerfully transformative. Used regularly, it will keep you on track with your life: Clearing and healing what you don't want and creating what you do want.

Healing Core Energies: A Guided Meditation, Zorica Gojkovic, Ph.D.—I created this meditation to assist in changing long-standing deep issues. It's a powerful guided meditation, albeit challenging. I recommend you use it only if you are very experienced with doing your own healing work. Otherwise, it's best to work with a therapist. A therapist who works with the body as well as the soul, in addition to emotional and childhood issues, is what I would recommend.

Attunement: Daily Meditation, Zorica Gojkovic, Ph.D.—A beautiful meditation to remind you of who you really are with affirmations for the best day possible.

Manifestation: Card Deck and Manual, David Spangler—I love all of David Spangler's work and particularly this manifestation deck. This deck is not a tarot deck and does not work like one. It is a tool of consciousness. Its purpose is to help you get clear about anything that's in the way of creating what you want and, in the process, possibly deciding your manifestation project is not something you really want.

Living With Joy: Keys to Personal Power and Spiritual Transformation, Sanaya Roman—A beautiful and inspiring book about spiritual truths.

Johnson O'Connor Testing Service—If you don't know what you want to do with your life or are seeking a new career, this service will test you, comprehensively—hands-on-testing to help you know your strengths, skills and abilities and how you generally operate in life. Highly recommended for anyone of any age to find a practical career path in life.

Dying to Be Me: My Journey from Cancer, to Near Death, to True Healing, Anita Moorjani—A phenomenal book about the way our thoughts create our body and a medically documented case of being terminally ill to being completely well instantaneously.

Proof of Heaven: A Neurosurgeon's Journey into the Afterlife, Eben Alexander—This is an amazing book that shows the connection between spirit and matter and, as with Anita Moorjani, a medically documented case of instant healing.

Spontaneous Healing: How to Discover and Embrace Your Body's Natural Ability to Maintain and Heal Itself, Andrew Weil, M.D.—One of the first books on holistic health and integrative medicine.

Buddha at the Gas Pump, www.batgap.com—If you want to expand your understanding of the nature of reality, just go this website. It has hundreds of interviews with spiritual people talking about all kinds of spiritual experiences.

For a huge amount of free resources, including a variety of wonderful and powerful guided meditations, go to my website: www.thetimeoflight.com.

About the Author

Zorica Gojkovic received her Ph.D. in English. Her dissertation is about the evolution of consciousness, mysticism and the new physics—as they relate to the novel.

Giving psychic readings has greatly expanded this original research into matter, consciousness and divinity.

By reading energy in their auras, she helps clients heal core issues, live their soul potential and experience the divine.

More information and resources are available on her website, www.thetimeoflight.com.

My Successful Manifestations

My Successful Manifestations

Notes

Notes

Notes

www.ingramcontent.com/pod-product-compliance
Lightning Source LLC
Chambersburg PA
CBHW030117100526
44591CB00009B/424